VILLAGES

BY AN

EMERALD SEA

AMERICA'S NEW RIVIERA. . .
NORTHWEST FLORIDA'S MAGNIFICENT
EMERALD COAST

True Tales of the Early Years

JAMES KEIR BAUGHMAN

2003

ISBN 1-932157-16-6

eBooksOnDisk.com and Moseley Hall Publishing
P.O Box 30432
Pensacola, Fl 32503
www.ebooksondisk.com

CONTENTS

INTRODUCTION

HISTORY, gathered and posed by one who researches ancient records, can be an arid, tedious affair... replete with dry-bone forebears, a flooding of dates, and places with names that have no color, nor vision, nor canticle.

History recorded in time to be penned by one who has seen and sensed and lived it...long abides as a song of life...exactly as it was, vibrant images sketched and hued in the printed, graphic word.

These fourteen short stories are of such..., living vignettes of the early years of America's newest Riviera, Northwest Florida's magnificent Emerald Coast.

Twelve of the tales are directly of the Emerald Coast itself. Two of them touch it only obliquely. "In The Tears of An Old Man," is of the time when the author was returning home, after an absence of only five out of more than fifty years. "The Last Casualty of World War II" is a story of the United States Air Force, so splendidly a portion of the Emerald Coast, and it's history.

A saga recorded in such venue surely cannot cover the broad span of an age. Yet, it may paint in vivid timbre a man or woman or place or event shaping that era. I hope, to some extent, I have done so.

JAMES KEIR BAUGHMAN

DEDICATION

This book of historical vignettes is dedicated to my mother Iris Keir Armour Baughman. She was a vital, pivotal leader of our economic development during years when dreams and hopes and plans were born that matured and blossomed into today's magnificent Emerald Coast.

Gentle and unassuming, she would be the first to step aside, to give credit to others, to say that no one could have achieved such an accomplishment alone. That, without doubt, may be true.

Yet just as surely, from 1963 until her retirement in 1977, she lived and strived at the center of the whirlwind of ideas and effort that brought us to where we are today. She worked side by side, as Executive Director of our Greater Fort Walton Beach Chamber of Commerce, with other historic civic and business leaders now revered as Emerald Coast pioneers.

For most of those 14 years, Destin was included in her Chamber civic and promotional endeavors, a time when it's name was the Playground Area Chamber of Commerce.

She also served six years as an early Administrative Assistant to three City Managers and the City Council of Fort Walton Beach, and was appointed as one of the early official City Clerks of the City of Fort Walton Beach.

From the late 1940's Iris and her husband owned four businesses and several residential properties on the Emerald Coast.

Blessed with great beauty, grace, and charm, she was the kindest, gentlest of mothers, a hard working wife and homemaker, an astute business woman, and a dedicated public servant.

Her life spanned 94 1/2 years, from July 25, 1908 until January 3, 2003. Her children, her family, her friends, and the prosperity of our Emerald Coast have been equally blessed by her long, God-given, time with us.

THE LOWLY FISH
...THAT SPAWNED THE EMERALD COAST!

Though the thing they provided was central to our lives in those years, I never knew their names. I wonder if any of us did. Perhaps Pete Earley, who owned the store where they traded their wares for easy cash, knew them. Perhaps not. I never heard him say.

Maybe owners of the saloons where they traded the bit of easy cash for a thing central to their painful existence knew who they were. People whispered that they slept under Brooks Bridge at the end of Main Street. If they did, the salty tang of the air and the easy-going back-water of the sea called Santa Rosa Sound must have been like family. The cloying heat and humidity of summer, the chill of winter, would not be an easy life under Brooks Bridge.

But, ahhh, the magic of the open air..., to live connected, mingled with the scent of the sea, the sun and moon and stars of Northwest Florida's enchanting Spring and Fall! Maybe it's not peculiar that some think it's worth the lack of conveniences. The point is few of us, in those years, thought the men important enough to wonder who they were.

After the Civil War they called it Camp Walton. For many years it was Fort Walton. In 1953 the City Council thought more vacationers would come if it had 'Beach' in the name.

Truth is, though, the town doesn't have a real ocean beach, just the river-like shoreline of Santa Rosa Sound and Choctawhatchee Bay. The ocean beach is across the Sound on barrier sand named Santa Rosa Island, stretching forty miles west to Pensacola. What's more, our end of it is in Okaloosa County, so we call it Okaloosa Island. Confusing isn't it?

For a tiny town, Fort Walton Beach has always had far more than its share of 'characters' ...of oddballs and dropouts, drunks and easy women, con-artists and thieves, and a few, perhaps, even more hard hearted. To share it has been a strange dichotomy.

On one hand the majority ...fine, upstanding, hard working, church-going people who loved and built this seaside City. On the other, fast moving, free wheeling, party loving, pseudo-sophisticates who left little but trouble and heartache in their wake. Some came thinking they might profit from the moneyed military and tourist here-today-gone-tomorrows. And some did.

Others came here to the sea, to the quiet and the sun and the piney woods of Northwest Florida simply because they were tired of the way their lives had been. They hoped only for a sabbatical, for time and space to survive whatever it was that cast them adrift from the anchor of somewhere else. They craved a place where they were not known, where the reason for starting over again might be left far behind. To our surprise, many of them healed their lives among us, brought uncommon talent and effort and persistence to our pursuit of growth.

And those of us who were young then learned, perhaps far too slowly, that swaggering along with the boisterous, high living, hard drinking, womanizing fighter pilot types so abundant among us...was not a good thing.

To feel the charisma, the mystique of it we must peer backwards in time and picture Fort Walton Beach, so like it's neighboring villages, in those somnolent years.

You see, in the 1950's Main Street was a finite world, perhaps the length of a half dozen city blocks. The world ended at Brooks Bridge and the waters of Santa Rosa Sound to the east, and at Cecil Bass' Spindrift Restaurant to the west. We all lunched and dined and partied in John Georgiades' Liollio's Restaurant in that same building for years after the Spindrift closed. Sunrise Marine fills it, and the parking lot, with boats today.

From the Spindrift to Pensacola the traveler of those years would find little but piney woods and scrub oaks, the loneliness of an empty two lane Highway 98, a rickety gas station at Navarre, another at a place called Midway.

Across Santa Rosa Sound, on the barrier island, was a lot more of nothing, of quiet and sand and scrub brush.

Crossing Brooks Bridge at night was a journey into blackness, save one dim lonely-glowing beacon.

In that darkness, where the magnificent Radisson Beach Resort sits today amid a city of brightly colored lights, was just one naked light bulb. It's round green reflector dangled precariously from it's own electric wire.

That tiny oasis of light marked the weathered plank steps to the Tower Beach Casino, an already old and faded wooden boardwalk, perhaps a hundred yards along the beach. Under its splintery summer-time shade were a handful of small burger, ice cream, and tourist shops, open from Memorial Day through Labor Day.

Atop sand dunes just west of Tower Beach's boardwalk were ramshackle wooden beach cottages leaning into the sea wind. Tourists actually rented those rickety shanties because there was little else. Besides, Alabamians who'd been making summer treks to this delightful beach for years already knew what to expect.

In fifty years on this coast, I've seen the inside of those beach shanties only once. In the fall of 1955 I was invited to a military squadron party in one of them. I got there late, after the party was already roaring.

When I walked in the door looking for the lass who'd invited me, another one grabbed me, wrapped me in a bear hug and held on...well..., like a bear. I wasn't near as "hep" as those party guys, but I wasn't exactly stupid, either. I knew, in a room filled with two dozen young GI's and a half dozen girls, that one had to belong to somebody. Do you know what it's like to act innocent and disinterested while an alluring young woman gives you a potent, loooong-lasting kiss? You know the answer...self preservation is the first law of nature! Her boyfriend was drunk and feisty, but a head shorter. He jostled with his shoulder every time he got near for an hour or so. I calmly endured it...seeing no reason to be jostled into a shoving match. My ego was in good shape. Of six girls there, I had a date with one, was kissed by another. And the lady who invited me turned out to be the mother of two of my three wonderful children.

There were just two roads on the island in the 1950's. Highway 98 drifted lazily on past the shore of

Choctawhatchee Bay and across East Pass Bridge into the fishing village of Destin, six miles east. A narrow sand-drifted old road, where four-lane Santa Rosa Boulevard now lies, ran two miles west down the island to an abandoned, brick, World War II guard shack. Romeos used it as a parking spot in the years when dating and respect were still fairly synonymous words. The most boys expected from a moonlight beach ride, then, was a kiss.

Main Street, fueled by GI's and tourists, had more than its share of watering holes. There was Jim Miller's Flamingo Bar & Lounge, Leon Bishop's Bar & Lounge, Bill William's Indian Mound Saloon, the Rep Room Bar at Docie Bass' famous Staff Restaurant, and the Bar & Lounge at the Miramar Inn. Besides, the thirsty could get a beer at most any eating place downtown. The Magnolia Club and the Spanish Villa were more elaborate night clubs with dinner, dancing, floor shows, and strippers.

Until about 1950 illegal gambling was wide open in Fort Walton in flagrant violation of Florida law. In July of 1949 I watched a guy lose a hundred bucks in less than five minutes to a pretty girl rolling a dice cage in the Flamingo Bar & Lounge on Main Street. A hundred bucks was a lot of money then. There were slot machines in almost every business bathroom in town. The Sheriff and local money-making muckety-mucks slyly looked the other way until a trouble-making Miami newspaper reporter blabbed it all over Florida. Then all hell broke loose, but the gambling didn't stop. It just slowed down and went more-or-less underground. Local gamblers always knew where it was. During the mid and late 1950's there were a number of gambling raids on bars and night clubs. Even the Elks Club lost a bunch of slot machines to police confiscation. That was a bit of a shock because everybody who was anybody belonged to the Elks Club.

It was during my tenure on Fort Walton Beach's City Council in the mid 1970's and '80s that the watering holes were shut down at 4:00 a.m. to dry out the live-it-up crowd for a few hours. Before that, after most bars closed at 1:00 or 2:00 a.m., serious party-ers would adjourn to Bill William's Indian Mound Saloon and party 'til dawn.

4

The next stop was a short walk down the block to Joe & Eddie's Restaurant for grill-scrambled eggs, bacon, ham, sausage, grits, hash browns, homemade biscuits, toast, orange juice, and coffee. In the bleary light of dawn, all night revelers were likely to be foggy, hurting, discreetly in need of hot coffee and solid food. For half a century or so, Joe Palazzo's place has been famous for the best breakfast in town.

It wasn't just the all nighters who might see them. In those years businessmen and women could gather for a sunrise breakfast at Paul Roberts' downtown Rexall Drug Store or at Pop's Restaurant a couple of doors down the street. In either case, it was in the early hours after dawn that those sad men could be seen walking along Main Street, turning south between the buildings toward Brooks Street, crossing grassy lawns between homes, to the shore of Santa Rosa Sound. Their shoes had cracks and run-down heels, their pants were filthy, shirts tattered, faces scraggly and unshaven, hair matted and oily. Over their shoulders they carried a cast net, carefully, professionally hung.

You see, in those small-town years it was a fish, the lowly Mullet, which was often the center of our social lives. When we had backyard gatherings we deep fried Mullet and hushpuppies. When we staged political vote-getters or community fund raisers we held Mullet fries. In the early years of the Billy Bowlegs Festival on Labor Day we closed off Main Street - to hell with through traffic on Main Street's Highway 98 - rented a band and held a street dance. We fried the Mullet around the corner on Perry Avenue in front of the Playground News office. In the decades since, that little newspaper has grown into the powerful Northwest Florida Daily News we know today. Back then fun and entertainment was not a costly thing. We could buy Mullet in the fish houses for ten cents a pound.

Our visitors, the military and tourist here-today-gone-tomorrows, laughed at the Mullet and at us. They called us Fishheads, and our newspaper the Fishhead Gazette, or the Mullet Wrapper on a better day.

But, there's a secret we never told outsiders. There are a few glorious things local folks should keep to themselves. Mullet, if deep fat fried and eaten on the very same day it's caught, is a rare delicacy, a veritable feast for the Gods. There's just no fish so mouth-watering to the taste, and that includes the strips of deep fried Mullet roe in spawning season. On the second day the Mullet won't hurt you, it just doesn't taste wonderful anymore. In the 1950's and 60's no fish house clerk or restaurant waitress would dare lie about the same-day freshness of the Mullet. We'd know the truth on the first bite.

So...now you know why those poor, sad, men were so important to our lives in those years. But the saddest thing is this. After an hour or so with their cast nets on the shore of Santa Rosa Sound, they would walk again across the grassy lawns to Brooks Street, between the stores back to Main Street carrying cast nets, heavy with Mullet. They would go into Pete Earley's Fort Walton Ice & Seafood and sell their catch. It was a short walk across the street to the Flamingo Bar or down the block to Bishop's Bar & Lounge where a dollar or so would buy a fifth of Muscatel wine or a half-pint of rot-gut whiskey.

In a little while, anyone walking along Main Street might see them lying on the ground in the weeds, next to some building a few feet off the sidewalk. They were drunk and dead to the world until the sweltering noon brought them staggering to their feet.

They weren't the only Main Street friends, though, who were caught by the terrible disease. Others among us, well known, affluent, successful, tippled there lives away. Strange, perhaps, the things we remember as time goes by.

There were always a few selfish folk who raged against the City Council's vote to spend fifty cents per capita a year of their tax dollars to fund our -then brand new - local alcohol treatment center. Most were here-today-gone-tomorrows until they retired...suddenly enamored of Northwest Florida..., and hoping we'd forget they weren't real Fishheads.

It seemed to most of us, though, that six thousand dollars a year out of a twelve million dollar City budget was a sensible investment in the humanity of our people.

As the gathering ghosts of years have drifted past on

sea-winds of time, I've often wondered who those sad, quiet men were and what ever became of them. In their agony, they gave us so much.

It's easy to look back now and see how the fried Mullet and hushpuppies contributed to what we are today. Those were the years when the few of us could only dream of the growth and affluence that now pours like golden lava over Northwest Florida, our Emerald Coast.

We couldn't know then, though, that we were rushing away from a time that now seems splendid to those of us who shared the small-town peace and quiet, and lonely beaches that stretched on to the sunset.

Now, its pure luck when you can find first-day fresh Mullet anymore, and with the new fishnet law it's getting worse.

The clerk at the seafood house or the restaurant waitress will lie to you about Mullet's same-day freshness in a heart-beat.

But...trust me on this one!...there are still a few of us around who know the difference.

In The Tears of an Old Man

He was not tall, perhaps four or five inches over five feet. His movements were rarely hurried, yet strong and purposeful.

Though slightly built, he worked with an easy energy that ignored the sum of his seventy three years. It was a subtle thing in his walk that hinted of tenacity. Few men of his stature would have a stride so long and determined. In that forceful pace his arms were held near unmoving at his sides, perhaps an expression of self control that had borne him grandly through many, many years.

By that time an automobile was not part of his life. In fact, he never mentioned having one...ever. He walked six blocks to work each morning and home again in every season of that stern Pennsylvania climate. In heavy snow-falls of three bitter winters he and I were the only employees in our department who made it to work. Neither of us knew the store would be closed on those snowy days. Neither of us had a phone. I couldn't afford one. He was careful with his money.

Despite his age he worked a five day, forty hour week readily matching effort and sales with those who were far younger. He'd done so in that same fine department store for fifty years.

It was in the fall of 1963, that I met Roscoe Sloyer, three months before our nation was stunned by the assassination of President John F. Kennedy. Long careers were a tradition at Orr's of Bethlehem then, not long before the celebration of the store's hundredth anniversary. Al Moyer, general manager, had worked in the granite gray building for forty five years. Russ Erdmann, personnel manager and fine clothing salesman, had been there nearly as long. It was an upscale store, widely respected for fashion and quality. Many employees had been a part of it's success for thirty years or more.

And many, like Roscoe Sloyer, bore grand old Pennsylvania Deutsche names, strange sounding to one from

English heritage of the deep South. As I came to know those self reliant people their names became symbols of strength and honor and integrity.

It was years before I knew that my own family - trekked westward with the expansion of America to Ohio, Indiana, Missouri, then far south to Florida - was rooted in the same sturdy ancestry.

I'd long resisted a move to the Lehigh Valley, the heart of America's Pennsylvania Deutsche country. Slower southern ways, I thought, would leave me a misfit in a loud, aggressive "nawthun" lifestyle. It was a revelation to find a thing so opposite. Truth was, friends I found in Bethlehem and Allentown were people of the land, much like rural and small town "suthunahs". As we might say down south, they "tawked diffrunt", but moved at a pace that suited me. The openness, courtesy, and dignity that ordered the life I'd known was as much a part of them as the "code of honuh," the pride of the old South. Their word was their bond. There was no need of a contract to get them to do a thing they'd promised. I'd find them patiently waiting, thirty minutes early for an appointment.

Moving there was a time of fear and withering hope. I found the job at Orr's of Bethlehem only after a weeks-long, door-to-door search to find a retailer who needed a buyer or department manager. Yet, it began a three year journey which reworked the fabric of life and sent me on richer in talent, vastly more humble toward those who share the burdens which carry us toward success.

As we make this journey together, life is a roller coaster, a whirling tempest of high and low, failure, success, happy times and sad, fear and confidence. Three fleeting years in the mid 1960's, frozen in the time warp of memory, were a compressed, accelerated vignette of those things, of life's larger canvas. A decade marched on before I looked back and saw the time as a major turning point, one that all of us navigate at some deep river crossing of our lives.

It was a wandering toward achievement, of searching for the place where business skills could grow, earn a better life for a young family. Heady success was a part of it. My management style improved the bottom line of a department my boss, Al Moyer, had managed for more than four decades.

He and I made the first buying trip together, and many others afterward. It seemed curious to find New York City just ninety miles away. I rubbernecked at skyscrapers like every rube, peered down into concrete canyons from high in the Empire State Building, was jostled in a gulf stream of humanity on 34th street. Soon, I knew 1290 Avenue of the Americas, 417 Fifth Avenue, and the Rockefeller Center as lofty friends.

Perhaps the biggest surprise was to find that Al, with his 55 years, could walk my thirty year old legs to knee-buckling weariness on Manhattan's crowded avenues. I rode the old Hudson River ferries, ogled down river to the Statue of Liberty, awed by the familiarity of things I'd never seen except in movies and television. Al and I flew back from New York, one trip, with Fordham Bixler, Orr's president, in his twin-engine plane. Fordham's 17 year old son flew much of the way, quite well for one so young. We dropped to a thousand feet and circled the newest Orr's store under construction in Phillipsburg, New Jersey, just across the river from downtown Easton, PA.

It is human to take for granted others who shepherd us in this rushing sea of existence, ones who share our time and our journey, who know the world as we know it. Reflections of those friends have lingered far more than others. They were comfortable among their own, yet willing to accept a stranger in their lives. It's not a thing one forgets.

Ray Paul was Orr's maintenance supervisor. An ex-racecar driver, stocky, hard-headed, tough talking, Ray seemed to enjoy cloaking himself in the aura of "Mr. Tough Guy." His poorly kept secret was that he was a pussy cat when anyone needed help.

Agnes Seneca, charming, graceful, competent, was my department's assistant manager. Her friends were a multitude among Orr's customers and employees. It was easy to see why. Agnes was first and always a friend to others. So much of her pride and happiness was in her husband and son and daughter.

10

Henri Bodder, a big, gentle, quiet spoken man was Orr's advertising manager. He called himself the French Pennsylvania Deutscheman.

Joan Moyer, women's fashions assistant, brought a sense of cooperation and relaxed friendliness to a department whose management was feared because of hostility and intrusion into other departments.

Russ Erdmann should have been a stand-up comedian. Wherever a peal of laughter was heard, you'd find Russ poking a finger with the punch line of his latest, sometimes hilariously risque, joke. That fine man was ever as quick with a pat on the back, a word of encouragement to those who needed it.

Aldo D'Agostino, Orr's Italian tailor, learned that trade from his father in Milan. How often I watched from the wide bank of windows in his upstairs tailor shop as snow fell into the winter gray pall of Bethlehem streets.

Fordham Bixler, whose family owned the three retail stores was Orr's president. His Yale intellectualism seemed as out of place in the rough and tumble world of retailing as it did in the pilot's seat of his Piper Aztec. He seemed very good at both.

I've never met a more capable or hardworking business leader than Al Moyer. Much more than a good boss, he was a good friend and mentor.

And then, there was young Eddie Haser, fresh out of high school, capable, confident, eagerly looking for his place in the business world. Perhaps I was his mentor. I steered him out of retailing, toward a career at Bethlehem Steel where he could expect good pay, training, stability, growing vacation time, good fringe benefits, and a meaningful retirement. In those years retailing, even in fine department stores like Orr's, was quickly declining as a place for a rewarding career.

Life's milestones, both joyous and chastening, often become permanent markers still seen decades later in the rearview mirror of our lives. Jill Marie, my beguiling middle daughter, was born in the Lehigh Valley in February of 1964, just after a thirteen inch snowfall. Son James set the pattern for flourishing school years in the kindergarten of a Lehigh Valley school.

In an unfamiliar "nawthun" economy, earnings higher than any of my peers turned out to be barely adequate for a family of four. I learned, the first bitter winter, how it feels to take an old hand-me-down wool topcoat from an observant, caring neighbor. A sweater under an unlined cotton raincoat couldn't keep out icy cold in zero weather, while I scrimped to pay the doctor for a daughter's birth. It was a time to learn the stomach-churning unease parents feel when mothers work and small children must be shunted to daycare providers.

One frigid night after Orr's closed at 9:00 p.m., I found my car towed away. Three feet of snow blanketed everything, and I'd parked next to cars so deeply buried I was sure they wouldn't move 'til spring. A Floridian is not likely to know much about clearing a mountain of snow from the family car. Bethlehem police didn't care whether a newly arrived Southerner understood traffic rules in blizzard conditions. The forty dollar fine was a shock to a family budget already stretched thin.

Management always brings tough lessons. But I worked with eagerness and drive that brought about a terrific career step-up to buyer and departmental merchandiser for all three stores. The promotion added Orr's of Easton, Pennsylvania and Orr's of Phillipsburg, New Jersey to my responsibility. It seemed a Mount Everest of youthful achievement, a new assured future.

Trouble that made mockery of accomplishment, and blew away that future, came without warning. Orr's president - I was never sure why - felt I'd made a mistake. The issue was certainly minor, and entirely within my responsibility. Yet, while I was away on a weekend vacation with no chance to explain, he took away the promotion and all its benefits. What he thought to be an error was really a purposeful decision on my part, designed to end markdown losses for the store. Oddly, inexplicably, he refused unswervingly, doggedly, to believe my explanation.

Reared in the ways of small Southern towns, where character is known, and usually taken at its word, that disbelief was gut-wrenching. Far more, it was profoundly puzzling. Why, would an intelligent corporate president make an impulsive, uninformed decision, then unyieldingly refuse to accept a straightforward explanation?

And, there was another baffling thing. Even in youthful years, I'd tried as well as I knew how to rely on God's guidance, especially in major life events. Why would He let such a thing happen?

To be sure, there was a stunning, wondrous answer to those life-changing questions. It came, though, only in a long, long span of years..., time enough to look far back..., to see the full forging of God's larger plan.

That "unfair" decision moved us on to a wonderful job, one that came without the asking. It brought the step-up to top management I'd dreamed of..., and fifty percent higher pay.

Far more, it brought us home to a place we've loved for more than three decades, a place of brilliant sunshine and glistening shores, where the wind blows clean and fresh from Northwest Florida's emerald sea, where my children have grown tanned and strong to adulthood, where I've found years of business success and public service, where I've made a contribution to the quality of life around me. Life's "unfairness" is sometimes an omen, a guidance. It's path may be winding, even tortuous..., but it may come tenderly wrapped in God's blessing.

And so, in Bethlehem, late in October of 1966, the time came to leave those who'd shepherded me, day by day, through three tumultuous years.

Among them, of course, was Roscoe Sloyer. But the quality of our friendship seemed different from the others. Though I genuinely liked him, there seemed a bit more distance between us. He was quiet, often more reserved than other friends. Sometimes he shared a funny story, never the smooth jokester Russ Erdmann could be. He talked about sales and customers and inventory needs but not with the depth or intensity of Al Moyer. His old friends came to shop, and the warmth and gladness in their meeting was good to see. But the high gaiety and chatter of Agnes Seneca's greeting was not Roscoe's way. In spare moments, we talked of many things; of local news, of business and world affairs, of store gossip, of our mutual love of reading. In those three years I never met Roscoe's son, a dentist, nor his daughter who'd married a successful professional man. I felt I knew them, though, through the glow of pride in his eyes when he spoke of them. Parents, of any age, share that so easily.

I told just three of them when I gave my two weeks notice, the ones who had to know in order to prepare. I hoped to stave off the pain of leaving, crowding emotion into a manageable span of the last day or so.

If that news could have been shared with others, Roscoe Sloyer would have been the last. The elderly, it seemed to me in those naive years, were different, barely touching the world of the younger, encased apart in their own quest, life-drained of emotion.

I was sure old people were so accustomed to the ebb and flow of things, to the coming and going of people around them, that it mattered little to them who came or went. Despite the hundreds of hours we'd spent together in a tiny universe of suits and shirts and ties and socks, I was sure that Roscoe Sloyer would be untouched by my going. After a bit I presumed, perhaps a month or two, Roscoe Sloyer would not even remember my name.

It was late in an October afternoon, three days short of my last day. The sun was low, rays weak and yellow, already hinting of the coming winter. Day shoppers had gone. With suppertime near, evening customers were not yet coming in. Stillness had settled over the menswear racks and counters of Orr's.

I remember Mary's lustrous silver hair, the quiet dignity and competence with which she worked, but her last name has wandered from memory in more than thirty years. She was manning the cash register desk "up front", as we termed it.

Roscoe and I were working together, tagging a new shipment of suits, far in the rear of the long, narrow, pale green department.

"Vell, Chimmy", I heard Roscoe's voice behind me. There were many, then, of the old timers who still clung to the ancient Pennsylvania Deutsche accent. Their "v's" were pronounced like "w's", "w's" like "v's", and "J" sounded like "ch".

14

"What is it, Roscoe?" I tossed the words over a shoulder, not bothering to turn around to speak, to look at him. I was a busy guy, pushing to get important things finished before I moved onward and upward.

Besides, what difference did idle talk make, anyway? Roscoe didn't know I'd be out of the picture in a few working hours. He'd have a new boss, and life would roll on among these "nawthun" friends as it had before I came, quickly hiding the space that "Johnny Reb" had filled.

"...Its...its about time...isn't it?"

It was far more than the odd huskiness in Roscoe's voice that stopped my hands in their busy motion. Another sound, an even odder sound, brought me to full attention, to acute awareness of the small, old gentleman who was speaking to my back. It was a strange sound among men, a wetness, almost...almost like a sniffle...?

"Time for what, Roscoe?" I turned slowly, puzzled, to face him, to look downward from a height of more than six feet to the familiar countenance of that kind, gentle, old friend. His weathered face was drawn tight, choked with emotion, with the thing he was trying to say.

And there were tears. Not mistiness. Nor a drop of dew at the corner of an eyelid. Tears flowed, flooded down his cheeks in a torrent that red-rimmed his eyes, made his breath uneven like a hurt child. The salty rush on his face was such that he pushed old-fashioned horn rimmed glasses up onto his head. With suntanned, age-gnarled fingers he brushed again and again at that wash of tears.

In awed, clumsy quiet, I stood, watched..., stunned. He tugged a handkerchief from a hip pocket, fumbled to find his face with it's alabaster softness. For a moment his eyes were covered by the white cotton as he mopped the wetness away.

With downcast measured pace, awkwardness, a biding of a moment more, he drew the glasses from his forehead so he could look up, see fully into my face.

"Vell, Chimmy", Roscoe Sloyer said to me, when finally he could speak, "it's about time for you to go, isn't it?"

PASSING THE TORCH
...IN THE GREAT NORTHWEST!

Perhaps it's growing wisdom, not gathering years that gives us grace to understand what we learn from those who shape our lives. Yet few of us learn quickly enough to profit from that insight. "Too soon old, und too late schmart", was the way the Pennsylvania Deutsche put it.

In the fall of 1956 our dream that it would be a daily was far in the future, barely believable. In those years Florida's finest weekly was on the corner of Perry Avenue and Brooks Street a block off Main in downtown Fort Walton Beach. The offices of the newspaper already seemed old, painted inside and out in a sickly pale green like the military hospital a few miles away at Eglin Air Force Base.

At 6'1", I've looked up to few men in my time, but he was taller, with a rangy build like my own. He was a thing rare among us, a true native of Northwest Florida. He grew up on a small farm near Sopchoppy and Crawfordsville in sleepy, forested Wakulla County south of Tallahassee.

Until you knew him well, his ways were a study in contrast. About him was the aura of his rural beginnings; a lack of hurry, a slowness to speak, an inherent disinterest in formality, near painful shyness. But, there was an easy erect pride in his bearing, strong craggy features, a hawk-like profile that reminded me of an old sailing ship captain.

It was his voice that revealed the fullness of his personality, of the real man underneath the facade given us by our growing. In genteel baritones, precise pronunciation of words, the depth of his education and culture and literacy shone forth. A mark of that culture, of the gentleman of the Deep South, was unfailing courtesy and a reserved court-liness toward women.

He tended toward reticence. Laughter was slow to light his face. But when it came there was a mischievous gleam in his eyes that spoke of good humor, friendliness.

In him seemed a quiet sureness of what he wanted to be, of what he had become. His journalism degree was from Florida State University, but he'd also attended the University of South Carolina. He'd spent 3 ½ years in the Navy, and served for a while as a high school principal. As a reporter he'd worked at the Bradenton Herald, the Tampa Tribune, the Tallahassee Democrat, the Chicago Daily News, and as editor of the Suwanee Democrat in Live Oak. All of this after beginning his news career with the tiny Havana, Florida Herald, not far from Tallahassee.

By that fall of 1956, barely in his mid-thirties, Wayne B. Bell was one of the best journalists in Northwest Florida and the Editor/Publisher of our Playground News.

The outgrowth of that fine weekly, today's Northwest Florida Daily News, boasts a circulation exceeding 36,000 daily and 48,000 on Sunday.

In the mid 1950's we struggled to sell 5,000 copies in a good week. Despite our small size, the approaching Tuesday deadline was a frantic time. We often had 28 pages when the paper came out Thursday, and were just as often understaffed. That gave me, a young advertising salesman, the chance to write news articles, a "What's New in Business" column, and hope that the nagging urge to write might nurture bare-bones writing skill.

A lot of reporters used the unschooled two-finger typing style, the 'hunt and peck' system. But he had taken time to learn it right. At the old Underwood typewriter, Wayne Bell's fingers flew and words poured onto pulpy, light-green copy paper that scrolled up into the machine from a cardboard box on the bare concrete floor. Focused on those flowing words he became transformed, a part of his craft.

With an editing pencil he was as deft and sure as any editor I've seen. We both loved newspaper life. He never left it. I left when it dawned on me that editors and publishers were the only people making a decent living.

The Playground News had a great crew in those years. Bruce Ranew was both advertising and circulation manager; Dottie Maslow, receptionist and bookkeeper; John Bosworth was associate editor; and his lovely wife Jean society editor. Claude Jenkins was a natural-born writer who penned the popular gossip column 'The Town Crier', and handled advertising accounts with a flair for hand drawn, single idea, advertising layouts. We call them 'sound bites' now.

In old issues of the Playground News, in Claude's 'Town Crier', Wayne Bell's 'Bell Tolls' column, and my own 'What's New in Business" you'll find a record of the Emerald Coast's business and social leaders in the 1950's.

Claude wrote about them all, sometimes those who were where they shouldn't have been, or with someone they shouldn't have been with, and the poop hit the fan, so to speak. Later Jimmy Pulliam hired on as circulation manager and stayed for almost thirty years.

On Monday we worked from 8:00 a.m. until 1:00 or 2:00 the next morning with barely time to grab lunch and dinner. Tuesday was deadline panic. Wednesday was an all day proof reading trip to Pensacola. In the 1950's the Playground News was printed on the presses of the Pensacola News Journal. The John H. Perry corporation owned both and many other Florida newspapers. Braden Ball, publisher of the News-Journal, was Wayne's boss.

Thursday and Friday were easier days. With deadlines past, there was time to share, catch up, plan ahead.

The exciting thing was, the few of us were in the center of everything that happened, connected daily to the events, people and future hopes of our "Playground Area," which Claude Jenkins later named the "Miracle Strip".

Sometimes on Wednesdays, we'd talk over lunch at the old, elegant Driftwood Restaurant on Garden Street in downtown Pensacola. It was in that famous old restaurant that Wayne introduced us to his favorite dish, Oysters Rockefeller.

Wayne Bell was a treasure trove of facts and stories about Northwest Florida. In in the weaving of those tales, I began to see it as far different from the phony orange, Flamingo, and big money image of south Florida.

I saw, too, that Wayne was sharing with us his love of a region that non-Floridians sneeringly called the "redneck riviera", and south Florida smart-alecs labeled "the piney woods section."

To be honest there were a passel of bib overalls, straw hats, red bandana handkerchiefs, and bare feet on Main Street during the frantic June, July, and August tourist season. But you could find the same thing right here in Okaloosa County any month of the year. Our military friends brought a bit of sophistication and culture to the "Playground Area", but we loved those "redneck" tourists. They were a lot like many of us and the summer money they brought was the same color as ours. The day after Labor Day you could roll a bowling ball down Main Street and not even hit a stripper coming out of the Magnolia Club.

The Playground News May vacation edition was mailed to thousands of potential vacationers and Wayne wrote reams of copy bragging about the whitest sand beaches in the world and the spectacular color of the Gulf waters. "Sleep by the Gulf tonight", was the come-on our tiny beach motels advertised then with photos of dozens of Red Snappers hanging from the upper deck of Destin party fishing boats.

In the Spring of 1959 Wayne spotted a Florida Panther several times near his cottage east of Destin off old Highway 98. In talking about the wildlife and fishing and geography of northwest Florida he spoke of places I'd never seen...of Sopchoppy and Crawfordsville, St. Marks, Carrabelle, Wakulla County, the clear water of Wakulla Springs, of Panacea and Perry and Homasassa Springs, of Port St. Joe, Cape San Blas, of Appalachicola and its magnificent oysters, of big rattlesnakes, of Braden Ball's uncle Ed Ball and the thousands of Northwest Florida acres controlled by his St. Joe Paper Company.

And speaking of wildlife, Wayne and Bruce and I sometimes drove to Mack Bayou, just east of where Sandestin is now, to buy a bushel of fresh oysters. I stopped that when, twice, a stomach virus lingered for several weeks. Mack Bayou was in the middle of nowhere, twenty miles down the bay from small Fort Walton Beach. You see, even in the mid-1950's we were finding pollution in the seafood chain, and the waters, of our own Choctawhatchee Bay.

Wayne must have been called at home very early that morning, because Destin fishermen of those years went

19

to the harbor soon after dawn. By the time the rest of us got to work at 8:30 the photographs were there waiting for us.

Looking back at the mid and late 1950's issues of the Playground News you'll find the credit line for Art Menillo of Arturo's Studios on most of the photograph's.

Like Wayne, Arturo's work made a commanding contribution to our daily lives then, giving us the capacity to see, as well as read of the events around us. Carefully catalogued photos left behind..., thousands upon thousands of them..., have given us a wellspring of local history rarely matched anywhere in the world. Art left Fort Walton Beach and Destin for a high-paying job as a combat photographer during the Vietnam War.

He would find little in his camera lens more awful than his 8x10 black & white photo seen by the few of us at the Playground News office in those early morning hours.

There, in that picture, was the body of Captain Johnny O'Neill, disemboweled by a terrible explosion, clothing in tatters, face bloodied and pockmarked by metal shards. An arm and a leg were twisted unnaturally, blown asunder, all but separated by the blast which killed him instantly. His body was lying face up, near his boat, on the dock in quiet, peaceful Destin harbor.

The plastic C-4 explosive packed into a commercial electric drill he found near his home was new and rare then, available only to the military, or perhaps underworld hit-men. He had put the drill in his truck and carried it to the dock. He was holding it near his belt buckle, still bent forward in the act of plugging it in when he pulled the switch to see if it would work.

Investigators could not even be certain that the explosive drill was intended for Captain Johnny O'Neill. He found it at the street edge near his mailbox, not at his doorstep. There was quiet gossip that his good looks and dashing lifestyle might have made a husband jealous, or that he might have been running something illegal in from Gulf waters.

In nearly forty years since that morning his killer has never been found. That awful photo, shared by the few of us, never appeared in the Playground News.

Another 1950's Playground News story sometimes comes to mind...perhaps a reminder of how lucky we are to have something near a normal span of years.

Wayne Bell, as usual, sent Art Menillo to shoot the 8x10 news photo. It was a picture of a fine looking young man, just eighteen years old, eyes closed, face completely at peace as though asleep, long eyelashes heavy with seawater. His body, too, was lying on the boards of a pier, but it was in Shalimar in the deep cove inside Dixie Point where Shalimar Yacht Basin is today.

It was a simple mistake that had made his life so brief. He was operating heavy equipment, loading oyster shell from huge piles brought by barges to Dixie Point. His big front-end loader had flipped backwards into the deep waters of the cove. It had taken rescuers far too long to get him out from under the machine.

Decades since, I sometimes think of the years he didn't have, and strain to remember a name hidden somewhere in a 1950's Playground News story.

He was given many more years than eighteen, but Wayne Bell left this life too soon, a victim of demon rum that has taken so many good newspaper men.

He rests, now, with his mother and father back home in Wakulla County near Sopchoppy and Crawfordsville.

Here on the burgeoning Emerald Coast, we owe him. It's to Wayne that we owe the credit for laying much of the groundwork leading to the achievement and affluence we have today. In the uncertain, growing years he used his considerable writing skill and the power of the press to strengthen our developing military, business and vacation industries, to keep us informed, to make this a better place to live.

Even more, he deserves credit for laying the groundwork for the powerful Northwest Florida Daily News which still serves us as we round the millennium and head off into another century.

On January 28, 1963 Wayne Bell was appointed to the original Junior College Advisory Committee along with eleven other well known civic leaders to plan our first reach toward higher education in Okaloosa County. There was no

21

one better prepared to guide that effort. The result of the work begun by Wayne and his fellow committee members is our wonderfully successful Okaloosa-Walton Community College. It's brought affordable higher education to thousands of our young, as well as adult continuing education and better career opportunities for many of us.

Time seems to move at the pace of a drifting tide when one is young. It was years before I knew...and I can't place the moment that flaming torch, this passionate love of Northwest Florida, was passed to me.

It's not likely I'm the only one who claimed it, nor is it likely that Wayne ever knew he was passing it on.

In 1983 when ten years as a Fort Walton Beach City Councilman came to an end, I was puzzled by a curious, unexpected sense of freedom. Again, it was a while before it came to me that it was the same freedom Wayne Bell had known...the freedom not to be bound to one mere cherished place, but a citizen unabridged, unfettered, of the grandeur that is Northwest Florida.

I've been blessed to travel often across her breadth since those years, to lonely alcoves of emerald ocean and gleaming beach, to lakes and running rivers and piney woods, among scrub oaks and palmettos and alligators, to quiet country towns and bustling cities. I know her now better than most men.

There are moments when I've thought there should be statues of those like him, those who made Northwest Florida what it is today. But then, in my mind's eye, I see Wayne Bell's face, and hear again that familiar near-shy, embarrassed laughter, the slow no-no shake of his head... and I know that wouldn't be his way.

But then, perhaps a nice plaque somewhere downtown, near the elegant Northwest Florida Ballet Studio where the old Playground News offices used to be, might be a good thing.

22

THE BEST DAMN WRITER
ON THE EMERALD COAST

There were a few who whispered that he might be gay. Like all of us, in this smallest of seaside towns, I knew him well for nearly forty years until he passed from this life in 1994 at the age of 80. In all that time, I never saw or heard a hint that would confide such. If he was, it was a very private portion of his being, governed with decorum and dignity befitting any man.

There were, indeed, close friendships with lovely, gracious women. He was always nattily attired, with a sophisticated, debonaire way about him, and rugged good looks that caught the eye of many a lady. For them he bade imposing charm, regal courtliness, especially to those endowed with wealth or status of one kind or another. It is true that he never married, though several of the ladies heartily wished it.

He was a man who had the look, the mien, the aura, the smell...of money. That seemed to matter to him, immensely. Oddly, in fact, actually accumulating wealth seemed to matter little. Perhaps, like many of us who ply his craft, amassing riches was simply not part of his sagacity, despite remarkable talent.

There were many friends, golfing pals, among well known, well to do, Fort Walton Beach and Destin business leaders. They were key among those who bought the advertising that funded his writing..., and his surprisingly simple life style.

Others muttered that he was an arrogant son of a bitch. But then...isn't it ever so? Great writers, by the mere assumption of their eminence, always brandish the forte to kindle emotion in a reader... applause, homage, dispute, concurrence, controversy, vexation, and - yes - derisive anger. Even now, a half century later, letters to the editor of our Daily News slam, praise, sneer, question, argue with...today's choleric local columnists.

23

To be sure, it would have been hard to overlook the panache that brought such growls from those who did not know him well. Over many years observing his demeanor, I came to suspect that he secretly reveled in that reputation, flaunting toward others a singular mystique of disparaging, haughty superiority whenever he chose to do so. Frankly..., he chose to do so more than occasionally. But, then, to those of us who shared with him barely hopeful, emerging decades on this beautiful strand he was a personae far more notable in his flair for words.

Claude E. Jenkins..., in the esteem of many, in the genre he savored, was the best damn writer on the Emerald Coast!

That's not to say there weren't a number of other fine newspaper men and women. Wayne B. Bell, was one of the best.

There's a difference, though, a Grand Canyon abyss it seems to me, between the highly ordered craft of journalism and the free flowing brashness of creative writing. That, in no way, is meant as a slap against the world of fine news writers who bring us the latest events of each day. Truth is, many outstanding journalists, even with extensive writing education - of which he had none - never gain notoriety as creative writers as did Claude Jenkins.

Perhaps the deep, gut burning, urge to write, to ignore convention, to pen whatever flows to mind, to speak with the sharp-edged tongue of singularity, to "march to the beat of a different drummer," is an inborn, God-given, gift. And perhaps that is so...even among writers who are never discovered, nor lauded, nor understood.

The piquant chasm between journalism and the free flowing pen could be tasted between two weekly columns. There was never a doubt Wayne Bell's "Bell Tolls" column held to all of the pertinent rules of good writing. And, certainly, it conveyed welcome tidbits of interest. But even with Wayne's fine college education, a stint as a high school principal, and years of widely varied newspaper experience, his "Bell Tolls" writing held an ordered reserve, a starchiness, about it.

Claude Jenkins' "Town Crier" sang with sassy elan, with boldness, impishness, elegance, bedazzling description,

24

lashing sarcasm when it suited...with singular creativity.

The one who finds a special talent, and happily plies that craft for forty years, is a blessed individual indeed...whether or not it brings material wealth. It is a thing so many of us never discover, or fear when we suspect it.

Claude Jenkins found his in the "Town Crier," recognized it, and knew what to do with it. It changed his life and ours, placing him high among the best known in the growing years of our Emerald Coast

In aged issues of the Playground News, in those two weekly columns, and my own "What's New In Business?" you'll find a record of the best known people in the 1950's and 60's, those who worked to lay the foundation for the magnificent Emerald Coast we know today.

Indeed, though, we were not yet the Emerald Coast in those years. In our quest for vacationers, we'd long been the Playground Area of Northwest Florida as the 1950's began.

Claude Jenkins glorious, long lasting endowment was to brand as "The Miracle Strip" our part of the Playground Area, the magnificent seaside of Fort Walton Beach and Destin. Claude is why we have Miracle Strip Parkway, a holdover from years in which many things, like Bob Bean's Miracle Strip Paint & Body Shop, were named for our Miracle Strip.

The naming of it came in a sudden flash of insight. He was driving west toward Destin on old Highway 98. "I came over a hill, left the woodlands behind, and hit the shoreline," he said. "I was so impressed by the incredible beauty of the water and snow white sands I was thinking, my God, this is a miracle."

That hill, that sudden view of the shore, could only have been at Miramar Beach, eight miles or so east of Destin, where Col. Michael Grimaldi had a large, far remote, beach front home. For decades local folk called the hill Yellow Dunes. So many of us have had the same spellbinding encounter at that spot, a first glimpse of what is to come... miles and miles of glistening white sands embracing an emerald sea.

The legend caught fire among us, albeit slowly, as

with most new ideas. It was never surprising to think of our beaches as a miracle! We'd just never said the words before. Claude's idea, his penning of it, was a chic, classy, public relations coup, worthy of the highest paid Madison Avenue ad writers. He was never paid a dime. But the words resonated long, intensely, in the hearts of beach lovers far beyond our finite stretch of exquisite shore. It helped mightily to bring us surging recognition, and flourishing tourism.

To be sure, though, that was simply Claude Jenkins' most obvious claim to enduring celebrity. His novel inventive catchphrases enriched us persistently, virtually with every issue of the "Town Crier." Today's Sheraton 4 Points Hotel on Island beaches was then our fashionable Coronado Motor Hotel. Claude tagged it *"the smartest address on the miracle strip,"* and the slogan morphed into our daily native dialect.

Another, at first, seemed a modest, cavalier, crusade. In time, though, it verified the might of advertising and Madison Avenue ingenuity, even in a rustic setting.

The Indian Mound Bar was a diminutive, ramshackle, affair. It was owned by Ex Fort Walton Beach City Councilman, Bill Williams. The chalky, faded, stuccoed barroom nestled onto footings of downtown's Indian Temple Mound. A window at the other end of the mahogany bar peered out onto a sun glared or night-hushed Main Street. Far too old, oiled-wood flooring sagged menacingly as one stepped into mahogany paneled dimness. Tiny, long-exploited, bathrooms reeked of...well...far too many recycled beers! One mini pool table, abreast the brief row of bar stools, left precious little floor space.

Plainly, Bill Williams' somnolent little fishhead bar was far from a hangout of the rich and famous. Claude dubbed it *"...the best damned saloon on the Miracle Strip"* citing it often in the "Town Crier." It became renowned, crowded, as a late night spot for "beautiful people" after the more glamorous watering holes closed at 2:00 a.m.

Too many of us, in those years, tried to sashay along with the hard drinking, womanizing, wild-ass Air Force pilots, and party-party turistas, who blew through our town. At *"the best damned saloon on the miracle strip"* we could party on 'til dawn.

26

Holton L. Hudson was equally prominent amid us, a Mayor of Fort Walton Beach. With the abiding assistance of his lovely wife Henrietta, he was also CEO of our upscale Coronado Motor Hotel. In 1967 Claude Jenkins and Holton co-authored a wee book encouraging "how to think your way out of a self-supposed hell." It sagely and effectually advised on how to deal with the sense of inferiority with which many humans seem to struggle.

Claude Jenkins titled the text "Inferiority Complex Be Damned."

In his personal habit he was far from a profane man. Yet, in his writing, he knew the power of a nimbly chosen, forceful, epithet. Claude Jenkins, it seems to me, would fancy the title of this footnote to his extraordinary, enterprising talent..., to his eminent contribution to our lives and the growth of our Emerald Coast.

It was late in October of 1956, that I joined Claude at the Playground News. The paper was already one of Florida's finest weeklies. We were headquartered on the corner of Perry Avenue and Brooks Street, where the Northwest Florida Ballet's new studio stands today.

The office was shotgun style, long and narrow, the last in a row of stores in one large building. Our desks were painted sickly pale green, along with cinder block walls, concrete floor, and most everything else in, and outside, the office. The place was always pungent with the scent of rubber cement used to paste up our ads and news copy. Newfangled jalousie window panes parted sunlight - starlight on Monday nights - into arrayed rows of glass slats. Broad store-front windows and tall glass in the door made the office front intensely bright on sunny days. A waist high counter separated brief customer space from seven desks. In the back was Wayne Bell's small office, behind it a tiny toilet. A spacious storage room at the far back held years of past issues of the paper along with metal filing cabinets crammed with photos which would now be acutely historic.

Claude's desk, cradling an old Underwood typewriter, was just across the aisle from mine. For nearly two years we worked side by side. Mondays were frantic, stretching from 8:00 a.m. to 1:00 a.m. - or even 3:00 a.m.- the next morning.

The hectic pace continued through Tuesday's 1:00 p.m. deadline, and Wednesday's all-day proof reading trip to our sister paper, the Pensacola News-Journal, where the Playground News was printed.

Thursday and Friday were slower paced, quieter, with time to share. He was seldom truly expansive, but in those quieter moments, he talked sometimes of his un-common years before the "Town Crier."

And, peering over a shoulder as he worked, I gleaned the finer points of his colorful approach to advertising sales and layout design, and saw first-hand the agony and exhilaration of writing.

Like many newspaper men of the 1950's, Claude urged the old Underwood with an unschooled, two finger, hunt and peck style. He would peck a line, sit silent, unmoving, his gaze far away, lost in thought, elbows braced on the arms of the chair, hunched toward the Underwood, crafting in his mind the next words.

Only his hands moved then, brushing together, turning slowly one over the other...until the idea was complete and fingers reached again for ebony keys.

In the long years since, our weekly Playground News has become what we could only dream of then, the expansive Northwest Florida Daily News. How gratifying it is to reminisce that Claude Jenkins and I, aiding editor and publisher Wayne B. Bell, advertising /circulation manager Bruce Ranew, and famed photographer Arturo Mennillo, helped lay the groundwork for today's prospering triumph, the Daily News.

Before that time, though, a stumbling, an normous foundering, had severely intersected his means, nearly demolished his calling. But then..., let Claude tell you himself, his own words echoing one more time...published for our meager world in his "Town Crier," appearing in the Playground News edition dated Thursday, August 23rd 1956.

***DIARY OF A MAN ABOUT TOWN...** Seven hundred and thirty days ago I took my last drink in the form of a quick, desperate swig from a half empty, half pint bottle of bourbon and poured the few precious ones left down*

28

the sink in a hotel room....I had made up mind with the help of a gnawing conscience, and the honest concern of friends, to stop drinking... The jolting impact of the decision's importance hit me the following night in the form of a cold clammy perspiration...

I had been introduced to whiskey's friendship at an early age... and nurtured it through years of adventure and loneliness ....It helped me grow in stature and importance in the presence of others whom fate had better endowed.

But of late my friend alcohol having grown tired of fighting my battles, had turned against me and was fast becoming my bitterest foe. Lying awake in bed, alone and in complete darkness, trembling from the revenge of abused nerves, I wept in desperation. Could I do it?...

All my life I had never been able to shake, without the aid of alcohol, the clinging realization of being born poor and under privileged....

Acquaintances snickered when I began refusing drinks, but friends crossed their fingers and offered a sincere smile of congratulations each time I accepted a non-alcoholic substitute. The dry days began to lengthen into weeks, the weeks into months. Insomnia vanished and nights became a precious part of life instead of frightening nightmares. Food prior to now was a necessary evil which I avoided as much as possible. My appetite returned and a meal alone or with friends was an occasion looked forward to. The everyday chores became pleasures, work a blessing and the future a welcome challenge. Nerves, that had become so badly shattered at times I could not shave or lift a glass, began to heal and calm.

I still longed to return to the many places that had given me adventure, friends, and - yes romance..., but there was no money, no clothes, and worst of all - no nerve.

... during those seven hundred and thirty days I have uncovered a few dormant talents that I never knew I possessed. Prosperity, although vague, is visible in the background, and my most valuable reward glows brightly in the faces of my family who never deserted me during those lost years .....Other trophies include tolerance, an understanding of the problems of others, a better desire to live and, thank God, firm nerves that are straining at the bits to get going. When will I take another drink? Maybe tomorrow - maybe never! Am I ashamed of the fact that whiskey got the upper hand? Hell no! I once knew a prizefighter who was allergic to lipstick!...

Once or twice, long years after,... in the late 1970's or early 80's, Claude Jenkins reached out again for his old friend whiskey. But they were very brief episodes, quickly put behind him by the same fierce determination to live wholly, to succeed, to use his new found talent to it's fullest.

Even in those early years, our tiny cadre of "locals" was already flooded, with "come heres," but Claude Jenkins was a true native of Northwest Florida, born in Ponce De Leon near Defuniak Springs.

He spoke little, at least to me, of his growing years there, other than of his father's untimely death. His measured comment of it obscured the emotion. I never realized it was a water shed in his life, until I reached far back, read these words..., his words..., written in the "Town Crier"on Thursday, July 19th, 1956...

DIARY OF A MAN ABOUT TOWN... *I am not fully convinced that the generally accepted belief whereof a man can accomplish any-thing he wishes, provided his desire to do so* *is unalterable, is sufficiently sound to deem it unquestionable. For instance, I have been writing a book ever since the day a knock at a classroom door brought the soul panicking news that my father had just been killed in a sawmill explosion. I was not my father's favorite son, although I was the oldest of three. The few scant years I was aware of who he was, in relation to my existence, offered too little time for me to convince him that I would in time warrant what crumbs of affection he passed my way. From that day forward, I have had something to say.*

The week before, Thursday, July 12th, 1956 Claude also wrote of home with a bit of humor, yet touching clearly on the love and gentleness that must have been centered there...

DIARY OF A MAN ABOUT TOWN...*At home my mother and sisters entertain company under a spreading sycamore tree, and since DeFuniak Springs etiquette is a lot less than demanding, the spot is not only ideal from a standpoint of convenience, but it's cool and roomy. Sunday afternoon caught the usual 'widow club' holding forth under the tree, all talking at one time about personal trivia, while I attempted conversation on the latest issue of Look magazine. There's an interesting pictorial of the great poet Carl Sandburg in the current edition, accompanied by brief, explanatory prose as colorful as the subject matter. I pleaded for an audience: "Here is one of the really great men living today. There's greatness in the simplicity with which he surrounds himself. His abundant knowledge and understanding avails him sustenance while we, the lesser invested, grope for worldly things to afford us nourishment." A quick glance proved what I suspected. Two of the ladies were yawning!*

"Now listen," I demanded, "I insist that you hear this! This man not only writes great poetry, but he's an accomplished musician. The caption states that his inspiration comes from Abraham Lincoln. He says he lives and breathes Lincoln, that Lincoln is in his very bones." (Notice here, I passed the magazine) "There's poetry in his hands on the typewriter keys."...I paused for comment while a siren complained in the distance. Finally it came. "I wonder who's in the ambulance...?" was my token of appreciation as the ladies arose to go...

Claude Jenkins "Town Crier" was patterned on world famous Walter Winchell's column of punchy one-liners written about quotable notables. Winchell regularly featured stunning revelations about high ranking Washingtonians. In a tiny town, needless to say, everybody knows what's going on, so astonishing personal tidbits were rare in the Playground Area of those years. In his reporting, though, Claude cleverly made them seem so.

Few would admit it, but most of us eagerly looked forward to the "Town Crier" to see who might be mentioned. Claude tolerated a felicitous secret. His cavalier penmanship made it appear that only the haute monde, the "beautiful people," could possibly be noticed in his column.

In truth... he wrote of us all, whenever he spotted anything he deemed worthy of attention. Leading business folk, eminent civic leaders, the affluent, ranking officials, military officers and their wives, judges, doctors, lovely and gracious women, even an occasional Hollywood celebrity shared Claude's spotlight with clerks, waitresses, fishermen, bartenders, chauffeurs, and others struggling through mundane phases of life.

Those of us who were not of the haute monde well knew who we were. But when we found our name in the "Town Crier," we felt for a day that we were among the "beautiful people." I've often wondered how much those

32

occasional mentions might have inspired many of us to work harder, to plan more earnestly for our lives, to hope someday to earn our own place among more notable friends?

Claude Jenkins apportioned his "Town Crier" into sub-paragraphs, titled with amusement and nonchalance

> ...,The Bigtown-Bigtime...Hither, Thither, & Yawn... Scratch Pad...Meandering... Playland Pulsations ...Sunnyrama... Serenade...Au Revoirs and Hellos... Randemonium...File And Forget...La Triviata ...Playland Carousel... Incidental Info...What They're Talking About... On And Off The Boulevards...Touring The Town... Appointment With Playland...Guys And Dolls...The Bleary Go Round...The Weary Go Round ...The Dreary Go Round....Scribe's Scratch Pad...City Limits...On And Off The Beat...Night Watch... Town Tour...Marquee... Quickies ......Spot Copy...Con Gloom Err Ations...Overtones Under-played...Homefront ... Playground Bulletins...Playground Potpourri...Vox Poop...!

There seemed no end to his entertaining, inventive play on words. There were usually three or so of those illustrative segments permeated with scintillating one-liners covering his judgment of the week's Playground Area notables.

"Town Crier" usually ended with the *Diary Of A Man About Town,* space Claude claimed as his own, to write a bit of himself, his personal opinions and observations, his sometimes quirky rapport with our world, his outlook on life. For many of us, perhaps to a great extent, the *Diary Of A Man About Town*, week by week, column by column, opened the door to let us know the real, the far more profound, Claude Jenkins.

In Texas, according to a contemporary news article, Claude operated his own import business dealing in leather goods from Guatemala, and handled public relations for an independent oil company in Houston. It was late in 1951 that he came home to Northwest Florida, to the bosom of his family, severely ailing with his "old friend whiskey."

For a time, in the small DeFuniak Springs hospital, he "lay near death" as he put it. Slowly, though, he began to recover, to move toward a more normal life, serving from January 1952 until June 1953 as DeFuniak Springs chamber of commerce manager, as a clothing salesman after that.

Amidst those efforts he began writing as a columnist for the Defuniak Springs Herald. And by mid-1953 he'd published several Town Crier columns in our Playground News. They were likely unpaid or nearly so, because he occasionally mentioned needing a "real" job.

Those early "Town Criers," though, were not like the following cascade of them which made him locally famous...simply chatty observations, memoirs, much like the columnists we know today.

In December of 1953 the "Town Crier" paused while Claude became our Fort Walton Beach Chamber of Commerce manager. He followed Wayne Bell who'd resigned his Playground News reporter's job to accept the position. Neither lasted for more than a few months. Each, in his own way, was an unswerving, independent thinker, hardly well suited to the grist of a political appointment. Wayne went back as Editor & Publisher of the Playground News when his boss, editor Art Cobb, was promoted to a far more lucrative assignment. Claude's "Town Crier" surfaced once more in mid-1954, bit-by-bit, day-by-day, blooming, ripening into the whirl of notable-quotable savoir-faire that came to enrich our lives.

Far it is from an easy venture, even for one who knew him well, to pick one and call it the best. But the following issue of the "Town Crier" likely conveys the far reaching spirit of his writing, the reasons for it's effect on us all. It is here in it's entirety, so you may experience it as we did forty six years ago...Thursday, October 20th, 1955.

SERENADE... *Spot Copy: Our agents report that dignified BOB FRAZIER will be* *nominated to wear Fort Walton Beach's "Man of the Year" halo. He's the gent who successfully ram-rodded the new bank deal... Our Nu Yawk spot spotted CLIFF and SARA MEIGS strolling the great white way... The smartini set are gathering at Leon & Eddie's "Side Bar", where pianist Chuck Hamilton is fingering the 88... Friends of society's Ruth Mitchell say she's sizzling about the picture mixup that appeared in a recent Sunday edition... Sensational statistics: There have been 1094 light meters installed, 250 phones placed and a like amount requested in the Playground Area since January 1st!... The blond in the Buick convertible is BETTY BIGGS, a Tennessee import who teaches for the Perry Business Schools... People are humming Nat (King) Cole's melody, "A Blossom Fell," and they're talking about the brilliantly portrayed and grippingly dramatic motion picture, "Interrupted Melody"...Our new resident banker BILL HARRIS is fast winning friends and being influenced by Playland people...*

*   *   *   *

Hither...Yawn... *Luvve that Virginia accent of chawmin FRANCES HARBESON ...A Bay-view Lounger observed: "The reason I demand onions in my martini is because they have food value!". . . Humm . . . Eglin Officers and their wives are glowing over the new club innovations done by decorator BOB MARK-HAM... The doll dining with jet pilot "Skosh" Small Thursday morn at Staff's was his wife, who's visiting from Mississippi... Incidental info: The naughtiest exhibition of nothing this reporter has ever seen was done by stripper Jo Ann Duprez, who appeared at Leon's Lounge as "The Original OOH-La-La gal"...*

35

Booful mannequin BARBARA MALCOM femceed the fashion show at Eglin...The younger set's LIZ JACKSON seen dining veddy often with her handsome dates at the Spindrift... Our friend, the "Prospector" writes from out west to right the definition of a Bar Stool! We know, chum, but censorship compels us to vary slightly... Expect much-traveled ALMA CULP to return to the Miramar fold, any edition... Restaurateur BILL and GRACE BUTLER home from Canada via Niagara Falls. Second honeymoon?...

*   *   *   *

***AU REVOIRS & HELLOS...** PEARL and JIMMIE COX leave soonish for Cuba, the land of castinets and Cuba Libres...HERMAN SCHELPLER planed to the west coast, that wonderful land of smog!... The BOB FRAZIERS took to the Tennessee hills... CURT COMPTON flew in from Austria, thus ending four years of Navy life... The ED ANDERSONS (He's the American Consul General from Belfast, Northern Ireland) bivouacked for a night at Riveria-On-The-Gulf...Scattered rumors say Destin's ALBERT FOX is spearheading a move to erect a bay-side recreation center that'll cost a pile of ready - a quarter million, to be more specific! ... Dr. AUBREY ROBINSON and his smartly-attired wife ANN were Bayview Lounging with AUBREY METCALF and playboy-judge JOSEPH ANDERSON ...Engineer DENNY PARTIN'S new carriage is a Corvette, yet, that once belonged to the International set's Cornelius Vanderbilt, Jr... A tipster called to report that Mayor TOM BROOKS purchased a new Chris Craft. Unconfirmed, however... LIZ DRUMMER, the waitress is telling friends* *about serving famed writer Erle Stanley Gardner who dropped in after the firepower demonstration... The veddy wealthy Mrs. J. G. SCHERF is planning a westward trek... WCNU's BUDDY O'NEAL and luscious AGNES SHAHID are getting to be a habit... (One the Criah would like to form!)...*

*   *   *   *

RANDEMONIUM... *It's a boyohboyohboy for cement scion LOUIS WOODHAM and the Mrs.! Caught Louie rationing cigars in the Rep Room... Playland stunned and saddened over the sudden death of lovable Mrs. Michael Grimaldi... Houston oil operator Tom Payne told this correspondent that Playland is planted over a pool of oil (He's in on the Citronelle strike)... Hotel manager TONY BISHOP (He was formerly with the Miramar) blew in town from Bainbridge...Incidental info: There's a man's shirt decorating the window of the Beach Shop at the Grand Hotel in Point Clear, with a Bronzini label and a thirty buck price tag! In case you're threadbare..*

*   *   *   *

DIARY OF A MAN ABOUT TOWN... *I'm getting fidgety. I think often of romantic San Antonio with it's winding river, it's park with it's thousands of pigeons, it's lazy lackadaisical attitude, it's friendly, fashionable St. Anthony Hotel, and the charming Minger house that caresses the Alamo. I find myself driving out north Broadway toward the capital city of Austin. Turn right three blocks from the next stoplight, up the hill two blocks, then left again and you're at Mildred's house. "Rascal," the friendly, black cocker runs to greet me.*

But wait! Why are you going there? Mildred died three years ago. Jaundice overtook her in Mexico, and she died in an iron lung. Things won't be right without her. Head south for Corpus and pause long enough for lunch at the Plaza. Turn south again and head for Reynosa, Tamulipas, where you bicker with the customs. Pay them their "Mordida" and swing south again over a desolate, coyote infested 150 Mexican miles to Monterey and the "Grand Ancira" hotel. Demand a room with a balcony and sit back and let the majesty of Saddle Back Mountain seep in ... and dream, dream of other days, other times, other people, other worlds...

Claude Jenkins loved Mexico, along with the enchanting cities of America's west, Houston, San Antonio, Las Vegas, Los Angeles. He spoke of them now and then in work days we shared at the Playground News. It seemed clear, though, that his familiarity was far more with the historic elegance of downtown Mexico City..., far less the grinding poverty surrounding it.

Claude was never a boaster, but slowly it became clear that in his years before the "Town Crier" he'd lived in the company of immensely wealthy and famous people. The center of that other world seemed to be his close friend Bob Neal, multi-millionaire heir to the Maxwell House coffee fortune.

At the age of 15 or so, Claude left DeFuniak Springs to seek a different life, as well as to effect one less mouth to feed for his hard working, widowed mother. He traveled to Galveston, Texas and worked for an uncle who owned a dairy farm. Maturing into independence, he landed a job in nearby Houston's Warwick Hotel as a bellhop. The Warwick must have been a lavish, uptown, hostelry frequented by the rich and famous of those years. In the course of that work, Claude said, he met a number of internationally famous people and it was there that he and Bob Neal became pals. Claude told me that he and Bob joined the Army Air Force, serving together as young Lieutenants through World War II..

After their discharge, high living, traveling, and partying must have quickly resumed, rolling on unaltered by the stringent gap of War years. Claude hinted that not only were he and Bob Neal the closest of buddies, but that he earned his way by managing business, financial, travel, and personal arrangements for the wealthy Neal.

To be sure, we in the far-less-advantaged middle class often find it difficult to fully grasp that those who are richly endowed by the winds of fortune are also mere mortals ...in need, as much as any of us, of compatible, trustworthy friends. How dismal it would be, in the human scale of things, to lose such a friendship, just because the other pal is of average means. Clearly, to value such a friendship over the course of many years reveals much about the fine character of both.

In fact, real attainment in our lives, attainment such as Claude Jenkins realized, can only be based on character,...character that springs from twin foundations.

First, is the early nurturing of home, learning, parents, siblings..., family. Sound mettle never evolves from "family" money, although it is innately human to grieve that misconception. Sadly, it often takes half a lifetime to fully comprehend that it matters little whether one starts out rich or poor, whether the relationship with a parent may be exacting. What matters is the broad sense of caring, integrity, support, guidance within the home itself. His writing hints that, like many of us, Claude Jenkins did not fully fathom the bounty, the solid foundation, his family had given him until mid life. It wasn't that he didn't love them greatly. Quite the opposite, from the earliest years in which he could, Claude sent home money to help his widowed mother and younger brothers and sisters.

Equally fundamental are encounters of early adult years as we leave the familial home...the choosing of good friends or bad, the choice of work, determination to learn and grow, finding a purpose...and perhaps mentors...to light our way. Claude Jenkins' grand providence in his choice of affluent, learned, worldly-wise compadres added magnificently to lore imparted through earlier, family, years...adding a balance of self mastery and sophistication, through contemplation of others, that few of us have the opportunity to share. Perhaps it was the thing that soundly rounded out a talent he "never knew he possessed." The lone, lamentable downside was the presence of unlimited amounts of Claude's "old friend whiskey" in that high-living life style.

He spoke only occasionally of the "lost" years. Oh, there were clues in several of his weekly writings. But then one "Town Crier" column opened wide the door, let us peer into that time...to see clearly what it had been. Three weeks or so, before I joined him at the Playground News, Claude took a vacation back to his old haunts and friends. Let him tell you, as he told us in his own matchless manner...in the "Town Crier" dated Thursday, October 11, 1956...

> *HOMEFRONT...Your correspondent's absence from the local scene tabbed an additional 5,000 miles on his speedometer and treated him to some of nature's masterpieces which are so prevalent in the vast southwest. I must, however, for the sake of fairness, confess that a strange, exhilarating sensation took over the moment my course was changed to eastward. How exciting it is to leave and how consoling to return...*

*   *   *

> *VEGAS VENTURE...Now here's a town!...An oasis affording the traveler liquids in any strength the wayfarer can manage to handle...My host, coffee heir ROBERT NEAL, had a command post situated in the plush Sands Hotel in which there were three fox holes lined with eiderdown comfort. Crooner FRANK SINATRA, who was headlining the entertainment at this particular desert spa, occupied one bed, Bob and Yours Truly the other. After Frank's first show we went on the*

40

Town stopping at such well known watering holes as the Last Frontier to hear PEARL BAILEY ...The Desert Inn to watch ZSA ZSA GABOR gallivant...The Showboat to see KALANTAN strip...The Dunes to applaud the best show on the Strip, LARRY STEELE'S "Smart Affairs," an all colored cast from Nu Yawk...The Riviera to see and hear the sensational and incomparable ERATHA KITT do a number titled "If I can't take it with me, I ain't goin"...Other places to enjoy GUY LOMBARDO, JOEY BISHOP, HELEN GRECO, SPIKE JONES, MEYER COHEN ...This fabulous Las Vegas, a city devoted to gambling, glamour, entertainment...A desert town surrounded by mountains, Lake Mead and Hoover Dam ...A clean, modern city with enough neon tubes to bring about a midnight sunburn ...Bob and I fly west via TWA Constellation while a hired man follows in my Thunderbird...

*   *   *

A PARTYING WE DID GO!...*In Bob's Los Angeles apartment which he shares with playboy Nicky Hilton, the three of us flipped for "firsts" in the bathroom. Bob won!...He leaves and picks up my date - Beverly Hills socialite MARY HOWARD, the widow of Hal Howard, the onetime Vice President of MCA who was killed in a plane crash a year ago ...ARTHUR CAMERON, an old Houston buddy in his struggling days, the onetime husband of actress JUNE KNIGHT and KAY ALDRIDGE is giving a cocktail-dinner affair. (He can now afford such pleasures since his income is slightly over $400,000 per month, mind you, and even in blaze' Beverly Hills these figures are sufficient to command* *attention! Should they become otherwise, he has been offered $25 million for an oil reserve he owns outright - One which has never been tapped!)...Arthur assures me of my invitation by telephone. "You simply must come since the entire movie tribe is holding invitations"...I mentioned that my itinerary would grant the time!...(Ahem!)...I have attended some noteworthy clambakes, but this clambake out-clambaked all the other clambakes of the past...Champagne, scotch, bourbon, vodka, gin and gingerale quenched the thirst of a list of notables including ELIZABETH TAYLOR, GERTRUDE NEISEN, KIM NOVAC, JOHN PAYNE, JAMES CRAIG, PAUL BRINKMAN, Directors GEORGE STEVENS and WILLIAM WELLMAN, columnists LOUELLA PARSONS SHEILA GRAHAM, and MIKE CONNOLLY, partygoer and giver COBINA WRIGHT, SR., maestro HENRY KING, KING VIDOR, DOROTHY MALONE, VIRGINIA BRUCE, LLONA MASSEY, ANN BLYTHE, BARBARA RUSH, GRETA PECK, DIANA DORS, HELMUT DANTINE, EDITH GWYN, NICKY HILTON, EVA GABOR, FRANCES BENNETT, the oil heiress who landed the second role in Edna Ferber's "Giant", parking meter tycoon DON DUNCAN, SARA SHANE, NOREEN ASH, LEE SEIGAL, etc. etc. etc. ...And as a result of a couple of Houston visits I must now find someone to subsidize me for a Cuernavaca gaycation...*

Life's triumphs are often as much in overcoming as achieving. Twice in his years, Claude Jenkins utterly vanquished what seemed immense adversity. First..., perhaps a barrier more of his own mind than unshakeable, was the sense of "being born poor and under privileged." Despite it, for nearly two decades, Claude lived in a lofty cosmos of wealthy and legendary people, travel, luxury.

At the end of that personal era, down and out, fiscally ravaged, sick with addiction, he faced relentlessly, then subdued, the grip of his "old friend whiskey." At last, in the intense effort of it, he found the true, the integral, measure of his being.

One morning, I came to work at the Playground News and found Claude Jenkins and his Town Crier quietly gone. It was likely one of editor/publisher, Wayne B. Bell's, poorer decisions. Among his other fine talents, Wayne was a stickler for following the "rules." It was never discussed at any great length, but there seemed some disagreement over outside advertising work... something Wayne deemed a conflict of interest with Claude's additional Playground News advertising sales and design responsibilities.

As fellow employees, it was hard for us to condemn Claude. Except for our "boss," the Playground News of those years paid bare subsistence. It was a matter of urgency for most of us to accept after hours work when we could find it.

To be sure, that setback didn't hinder Claude much either. Oh, he floundered with a small, far less recognized writing career for a brief while. Then, about 1959, if memory serves well, he hit on the idea of self publishing, a venue in which no one could restrain his writing, or his resources.

Far from surprising to those of us who knew him, the little magazine was grandiosely christened "Status." In his maverick fashion, Claude held it's publication to no specific time table. Status "published occasionally" his Town Crier mentions for another 30 years, or so.

His work days were often lengthy. But then, what is work to the man who owns his livelihood, his own soul? In the Florida sunshine we'd see him near daily in the Fort Walton Beach Chamber of Commerce and many other community doorways, often in the famous Staff's Restaurant where so many business and Chamber concerns were settled over coffee in those years. We'd spot him, too, going in and out of the stores and offices of his advertising customers ... places where he gleaned untold numbers of his notable mentions.

Well into evening hours, we'd spot Claude sitting here and there, quietly, alone, snooping - he called it - in our grand dining spots and gin mills for lively accounts of the Miracle Strip haute monde. He'd be sipping from a small whiskey glass of brown liquid - always Coca-Cola - and smoking incessantly. We might find him in Staff's Restaurant or it's upscale Rep Room Lounge, the Seagull, the Coronado Motor Hotel, the Shalimar Club, the Bayview, the Magnolia Supper Club, the Yacht Club, occasionally far down the beach at the Spyglass Inn. He was a near fixture at the glamourous parties of the Chamber's Host Committee, virtually any other public social gathering, a sought after guest at more reclusive, private galas.

Indeed, in that splendid epoch of Fort Walton Beach's Main Street, he was a towering figure on his Miracle Strip..., our Emerald Coast of Northwest Florida.

Surely, it is one of the prices paid for the good fortune of a gathering of time. It's a strange sense when the grasping of it creeps first upon us..., the odd comprehension that we are to know the full span of years given to others who seemed timeless, stars, in our finite universe.

We learn a bit, perchance a great deal of their beginnings, their growing span. For a time, perhaps long years, we share a work-a-day world, know them abundantly, their dreams, hopes, aims, the force of their uniqueness.

Then, for a time, we're left to weigh in the balance of posterity the meaning of their days, their tithe to the "grand scheme" of consciousness we shared.

Somewhere, hidden in the lavish, meandering phrases of Isaiah, are words that strike to the heart of our mortal transience. I've read, and reread...but they elude me now. I wish I could find them again, for they speak poignantly, to the marrow, to the very essence, of his time among us.

"The winds cometh..." they murmur, "...and stirreth ...and bloweth away."

In Ponce De Leon, close by his Miracle Strip, amid quiet fields and forests there is a modest rural cemetery, a gathering of kin in their family plot.

Claude Jenkins rests there now from his splendidly fertile, triumphant, earthly labors.

And here in the old Playground Area of yesterday, there is a sense of emptiness with him gone, a paling of the air of savoir-faire he radiated. His commanding talent, his words, his sense of the aesthetic, stirred mightily indeed while he abided among us. He left us with a Miracle Strip, an Emerald Coast, finer, more fashionable, far more affluent, than when he began.

And too, Claude left a special legacy in his writing for all of us who love this beautiful coast as much as he did. The words are worth repeating...remembering.

"How exciting it is to leave...and how consoling to return."

THE LAST CASUALTY
OF WORLD WAR II

The B-36 'Peacemaker' was a mammoth flying machine, in it's day the largest ever flown by the U.S. Air Force. Wingtip to wingtip, it stretched 230 feet, as wide as the height of a 23 story building. It was designed and first flown as an intercontinental bomber, but it's propellers and piston engines were quickly surpassed by swift jets that could fly nearly three times it's cruising speed. The squadrons already in service were relegated, for a time at least, to the mission of reconnaissance, and the plane was re-designated the RB-36.

Just after midnight on the morning of Wednesday, March 18, 1953 RB-36H #51-13721 thundered down the runway at Lajes Field in the Azores, 900 miles west of Portugal, and took off into turbulent Spring weather of the North Atlantic. It climbed a scant hairs-breadth over ocean waves and lumbered westward toward the home of it's twenty-three man crew at Rapid City Air Force Base, South Dakota. Behind, following it's lead, were eleven more of the giant planes.

The General who led them had given orders that the daylong flight to the coast of North America be flown just 1,000 feet above the stormy seas. It was an altitude that gave perilously little room for error, especially in the terrible weather conditions they would find.

The obstinate, unswerving continuance of that order, in the face of severely worsening weather, proved to be one of the most rash military blunders of early post-World War II years. It caused the loss of two multi-million dollar bombers and 33 men, and came within a gnat's whisker of losing the other eleven planes and 231 men following.

The deadly misjudgement, quickly camouflaged by the highest of military honors, was not typical of the capable, hard driving officer. But, a half century later, a review of the formal accident report makes it clear that his action, or lack

46

of it, on that dreadful day made him the General George Custer of modern times. Like Custer, he was flawed in one awful judgement, yet esteemed, honored, memorialized in a manner which is given to few others.

Thirty-two of lower rank who died with him, because of him, have remained faceless, unknown. They, like Custer's 212 at the Little Bighorn, would never have chosen to die so needlessly, so young. The lives that were taken from each of them deserve remembrance. They all had a story to be told, but these words know only the moments, and hours, and brief years of one, perhaps the youngest and lowest ranking of all. The account of his fleeting earthly season is a symbol for all who were with him that day, a hallmark for so many who have been lost in service to our country...too youthful, too low ranking to be remembered.

Moreover, it is the ballad of life, of boyhood friends growing of age in the frightful span of World War II, eagerly looking forward to the coming years, dreaming the heady dream of flight.

"Yank-ee doo-dle went to Lon-don...rid-ing on a pon-eee", we were swaying down the hall as one, side by side, arms locked over each other's shoulders, bleating out words of the old song of the American Revolution. We had sung it in music class that very morning, but as we warbled into the lunchtime emptiness of our classroom we improvised bawdy words of the next stanza we'd learned from some tender-aged wise-acre classmate..."stuck a feather up his ass and called it maca-roneeee". We sang at the top of our squeaky voices, smugly sure we were alone.

Miss Warren, our first grade teacher, stood up suddenly. She'd been kneeling, hidden behind her desk. Luckily, she wasn't facing our way, but toward the scratchy slate chalkboard. Before she could turn, see who we were, we bolted out of the room, past the broad open width of Varina Elementary School's auditorium edged by it's surrounding halls. It was a short scamper down the hall and out the back door to lose ourselves among peers on the playground. That was about as bad as elementary school kids got in rural Virginia in the Spring of 1939, but, to be sure, it was pretty

47

sassy for first graders.

Phillip T. Mancos, Jr. and I became fast friends that first school year. It was friendship that never faltered during eight growing years of elementary school in Varina, the peaceful farm community on the outskirts of Richmond.

I wonder what it is that so quickly seals a friendship, what instincts within us sense the unseen, non-blood kinship that draws the unrelated into a bond like brotherhood?

I've wondered, too, over many years of this precious gift called life, what's in the bond that keeps the feeling of brotherhood close and warm and alive a half century after it's no longer possible to see, or hear, or share?

If physical attributes were the core of friendship, it must have been noses that drew us together. We were each blessed with proud, prominent honkers...such that strangers often mistook us for family.

And we were both fast. Phil was the fastest runner in Varina Elementary School and I was a close second. On field days, in the 50 or 100 yard race, we were in our element, running together like the wind. We were always within touching distance, Phil a breath ahead. I was a hint taller with long gangly legs and big feet. He was more compactly proportioned with little feet that flew.

In the lifetime between first grade and the eighth, I remember only once that Phil was not first across the finish line. It was I, that cool Spring day, who surged ahead at the last second and beat him by a toe length. To tell the truth, there must have been something amiss. Perhaps Phil had a cold or one of those painful styes on his eyelid. He got them often. It's always great to win against someone who's the best. Phil grinned and congratulated me, but there was a look in his eyes that told me it would never happen again. It never did. Phil didn't like to lose, even to his best friend.

In the second grade we shared one of life's lasting lessons. In a class play we were somehow picked to sing a duet. The "Indian Love Call" is a beautiful, melodious old song, a State treasure of sorts in the Virginia of those years. We were dressed in Indian costume with full feather headdress and stage makeup. Phil and I, smeared with lipstick and rouge, moccasin-padded out in front of the audience, into the high pitched oooooing and warbling of the tune, stunned to find ourselves the sole target of a couple of hundred pair of big, intense eyes. Phil, in his quietly self assured way, never said anything about it afterward, and I never asked him. My stomach did a half dozen flip-flops, and several high notes were little more than croaks. My mind was made up right there on the dark oiled wooden stage boards of the old Varina elementary school. The stage was not a place I wanted to spend much of my life.

We were both "A/B" students without trying very hard, and both tended to be adventurous. Like the day Phil kept pounding a 22 caliber bullet between two rocks at the end of the playground near the forest. I warned him over and over again it was dangerous, and shuddered with relief when the bullet exploded with a loud bang without hitting either of us or some other hapless kid.

Usually though, Phil was the calm steady one and I excitable and impulsive like a bubble of water in a hot frying pan. One late Winter day we rushed out onto the playground to find a sea   of mud left from the snow thaw the day before. It seemed like a terrific idea at the time...to race   f u l l speed into the mud, lock knees in an ice skating position, to see how far feet would slide.

Quicker than Phil could say "I don't believe I'd do that...", my feet flew up, high up! He stood there wide-eyed as I slid about ten feet on my back in three inches of brown ooze.

Miss Barrett, our third grade teacher, put mud-caked shirt and pants on the hot radiator to dry, and me in the only clothes available. It was Phil who reminded me it was my day to run the marionette show.

So, there I was, up on the tiny elevated stage in the classroom corner, in front of twenty or so giggling kids, wearing a yellow and red clown costume. Do you think Phil didn't laugh with the rest of them? If you do, you don't know kids. You bet I was humiliated, but there was never a question that Phil was still my best friend.

With easy-going ways, Phil got along with all the kids. His best friend's mouth was as impulsive as the rest of me. It

49

got me into a lot of fights over the years. Trouble was, I wasn't good at fighting either. For some reason I seldom felt "fighting" anger. Besides, even when I knew I could win, I couldn't muster the meanness to punch a kid in the face when moments before he'd been a friend. I like guns, can shoot straight as an arrow, but for the same reason I've never wanted to hunt.

One day our friend Harry Beattie decided, as we say in the country, that he was going to "clean my plow". About six other friends decided to help him. Faced with that - likely self inflicted - hostile group I impulsively decided to "abandon ship". Gasping with laughter at their clumsy pursuit, I raced away with wind rushing in my ears and leaped like a gazelle over a hedge as high as my head. I crashed through the hedge top to the ground, bounded across Elmer Kohl's plowed field, with our friends losing ground at every step.

Its amazing...the things we learn the hard way! By the time the school bell rang the next morning two of those hard lessons were crystal clear. In the many years since, they've meant a lot. First, of course, there are times we must stand and fight even if we know we might take a pounding. In 'grown-up' years we'll face things a lot more painful than a fist.

The second thing learned is more important. A friend...a real friend, that is...will remain your friend when you're down, when you're in trouble, when you've done something stupid. Phillip T. Mancos, Jr. shared the embarrassment of that impulsive, less than manly decision. On that awkward morning, he was still my best friend.

Some things that stick in the mind seem so trivial, I wonder why they're remembered at all. They must have some powerful meaning to the child in us. In the Virginia of the 1930's, for first and second graders, there was the Spring Maypole Dance. Even at the age of six, Phil and I hated clutching those pole-tied ribbons of colored crepe paper and skipping around in a circle. Worse, the Maypole was set up on the school's broad, green front lawn fronting right on Varina's Route 5 where anyone going by could see. We'd weave in and out until the wide ribbons were interlaced tightly around the pole and we were all dizzy. We thought the pole looked okay, a basket weave of bright color all the way to the top, but, to Phil and me, it seemed a sissy, embarrassing thing for boys to have to do.

We caught crawfish in a cold, swiftly running creek in woods at the edge of Varina's schoolyard. When we were older Phil built the framework of a very tippy little boat, at most six feet long. Its sides and bottom were just an oiled tarpaulin draped over the frame. The thing actually floated and we paddled It like two grizzled explorers in a swampy rain pond in a small wooded area just across the road from his house on Route 5 also called the Curles Neck Road or the Tyler Memorial Highway.

Starting in the third grade we played on schoolyard ball teams. We weren't sports fanatics like our pals Harry Beattie, Carey Garrett, Richard Reed, Herman Jones, William Megat, Frank Garrett, Dallas Oslin, Emory Palmquist, and Coleman Ragsdale. But, Phil played well, with easy, natural sports skills. He just never made a big deal about it. In fact, in later years he became quarterback and captain of the Varina High football team.

Seemed I was born utterly without athletic ability. I was so heartened to be chosen next to last - rather than last - for a recess team that our teammates groans of dismay were like a whisper in the wind. How much we appreciate a friend who's quietly supportive in times like that. Phil would look away, kick dirt with a toe, pretending he was not noticing as I waited and waited to be chosen. When it was his time to choose, I'd be high up the list even though he knew I wouldn't be much help. I was nearly thirty and playing golf before I discovered that athletics can be learned.

It was small, the size of a paperback book, but Phil's Johnson-Smith catalogue held a lot of our non-scholastic interest. I wonder if the company is still in business today? It's pages were filled with curiosities amazing and exciting to boys isolated in a rural area. There were magic tricks and magnifiers, telescopes and lightning generators. And, too, there was the twisted humor of stink bombs and itching powder, hand-shake shockers and whoopee cushions.

Aaahh...how Phil and I pondered just which teacher might suffer the most embarrassment from the raucous breaking-wind sound of a whoopee cushion secretly placed in her chair...and we gave a lot of thought to Miss Goss, our sixth grade teacher.

We never quite had the courage to try that one, though. Varina, in the 1930's and '40's was a society which would have dealt harshly with such an insult, and we knew it. Phil and I and our schoolmates grew up in the midst of a social heritage that was long and more than a bit stuffy. Varina is the community where the Indian princess Pocahontas lived with her English settler husband John Rolfe in the earliest years of our nation. It's the place where Thomas Jefferson's daughter Martha lived on a 950 acre plantation with her husband Thomas Mann Randolph, Jr. Many Civil War Battles were fought there and Laurel Hill Methodist where Phil and I attended church was used as a Civil War military headquarters. My grandfather, James Wilson Baughman built the main house inside a Civil War fort on the farm where I grew up.

Our lives, along with all Americans, changed drastically in the brief hours of one day...December 7, 1941. Phil and I were nine years old, but a half century later, the day stands out so clearly. My father often drove our family to Richmond's Byrd Field on Sundays. We would stand by the fence and watch mechanics in stark-white coveralls refuel gleaming twin-engine DC-3 airliners of Eastern Airline's "Great Silver Fleet". Those beautiful planes, engines humming softly with reduced power, glided over our farm fields every day as they drifted down toward landing At night we could see them coming from miles away, red and green navigation lights winking against the dark, star-twinkled sky. As the plane floated past, just a few hundred feet above our heads, it's row of lighted cabin windows could be clearly seen. For a few seconds those squares of muted light eased the loneliness and dark and quiet of the open fields around our small cottage. They spoke to us of busy people and exciting places and the hurry of a new way of travel...just as railroads had fascinated our fathers and grandfathers.

As we grew older Phil and I would sometimes ride our bikes the five miles or so to Byrd Field to watch the military planes take off and land.

Even as children, on that Sunday afternoon, we could sense a tension, an excitement in the air. It was a clear, mild day for Richmond in December. Two mechanics, white coveralls bright in the sunshine, were standing high up on glinting metal wings, pumping fuel into the plane's tanks. Their voices were loud, laughing, excited. "Where do you think they'll send you?" one asked. "I don't know yet. Do you have any idea where you'll go?" the other called back.

"What's happened?" I asked my father as we drove away from Byrd Field. "What were those mechanics talking about?"

He drove pensively, staring blankly ahead for a long moment before answering. "The Japanese bombed Pearl Harbor this morning," my father finally said quietly, "we're at war."

Bedtime for my sister Jean and me was usually a firm eight o'clock, but that Sunday night was different from any one before or after. Like millions of other Americans we sat huddled in front of the polished wood Philco table model radio and listened to news reports punctuated by crackling static so familiar to radio of that era. We opened a thin world atlas our father kept on the table under the Philco and pored over a map of the Hawaiian Islands where the death and devastation of Pearl Harbor lay.

The changes in our lives were immense. Even amid the serenity of Varina's rural life there were air raid wardens who knocked on the door and warned of slivers of light around blackout curtains. Those tiny points of light might give a target to an enemy plane. There was rationing, especially of gasoline and cigarettes and sugar and chocolate and meat. No civilian automobiles were manufactured in the years 1943, 1944, and 1945, and few in 1942. Clothing factories made far more military uniforms than civilian clothes. That brought books of ration stamps, victory gardens, changes in food and clothing choices, and severe limitation to travel. Our promised vacation, a mere hundred miles to Washington DC where our parents eloped to marry in 1931, was put off for the "duration" as everyone called the wartime years. After the war our family left Virginia for the deeper South and we never made that trip to the Nation's capitol.

In Varina, as in every community in America, it was with fear and pride that we watched our young men rush to serve their country.

He often came to mow our lawn before he was old enough for the "draft". Eddie Belknap bragged that his hound dog could catch every piece of meat thrown him, even from the high porch. That was, Eddie confided to me one lawn mowing day, until he threw the dog a piece of lemon. The startled hound never again caught anything thrown to him.

I guess its an odd thing to remember about a friend from so long ago. I was eleven or twelve when they sent him to war and Eddie seemed "grown up" to me then.

As a father, looking back toward those fearful years, I know now that he was just a kid...freckle faced, sandy haired, muscular, strong. A really fine young man. He was gone just a few months when news came that he had been killed in Germany. Eddie Belknap was just eighteen. These fifty years, the bronze plaque with his blue star has hung on the wall of the old Varina School.

The title of the Reader's Digest article brought a sudden intuition that I knew the story. Jack Elliott grew up in Varina and went to war as a bomber pilot. He was older than Phil and me, so we knew him only slightly. But the Elliott family was an important part of Varina in those years. His mother and father were good friends of our parents. Jack's plane was shot down over Germany and he spent many months as a prisoner of war.

There, fifty years later, in a famous national magazine was his daughter's story of Jack's heroism and his life after the War. There were details I'd never known, but there was a thing left out. Digest readers might not have understood it as friends and neighbors did, but it was a lesson Jack carried with him into manhood, into combat fear, and capture. Jack's father was a fine, capable, successful man who faced life head-on with a stuttering impediment that made talking awkward and difficult. It was not surprising to anyone in Varina that his son might become a war hero.

I don't know which of us first voiced the fierce fascination with flying. Even before Phil and I 'teamed up' in the first grade, there's a dim, early, recollection of a row of colorful fabric covered bi-planes, of talking with a pilot, of worrying that the pilot might have been the one killed when a Richmond Times-Dispatch news story reported a plane crash.

Our pals seemed far more interested in playing ball than war or aviation. Phil and I played our share of sports with them, but often we'd climb near the top of a pine tree and eat lunch from brown paper bags. The pine was small, with strong lower limbs for easy climbing. We were little more than twenty feet above terra firma, but two stories in the air seems high to lads of eleven or twelve. The tree was sapling limber and with our combined weight high in the top it swayed grandly in the wind...a bit, it seemed to us, like flying. For the span of a lunchtime we looked down on the world. Up there, in the air, we plotted our future lives as swashbuckling fighter pilots.

The famous, now antique, Movie-Tone newsreels shown in the school auditorium let us see combat and the weapons of World War. It was the wondrous fighting machines of the air that gripped our attention. Aviation was struggling to grow out of the wood and canvas, open cockpit era of early flight when Adolf Hitler thrust World War II upon us. Phil and I eagerly followed the frantic development of the modern warplane. Schools across America held classes in the identification of aircraft so every citizen might recognize an air attack. We memorized the planes of every nation. We knew their photos or silhouettes at a glance. The Me 109 and Fw 190 were German fighters. Italy had the Savoia-Marchetti. English pilots flew Supermarine Spitfires and Hawker Hurricanes that saved England in the aerial Battle of Britain in 1940. Japan's Mitsubishi Zero was faster and trickier than most of our early fighters. Others among America's air armada were the P-47 fighter, the C-47 cargo workhorse, and the four-engine B-17 and B-24 bombers that brought so many of our boys back from the flak-blossomed skies of Europe. Phil and I knew the planes that flew over the farm fields of Varina by their sound. A half century later, the roar of their engines, the whine of air over fuselage and wings, are still like old friends.

It was a new plane...the most exciting, the most beautiful fighter ever built that rammed full throttle to our dreams of flying. It was the middle of the war years when the North American P-51 entered the skies of Europe. Its power and speed and sleek nimbleness changed the face of aerial combat. Finally, we had a fighter to match the feared German Me 109. More important, we had a fighter that could escort bombers all the way to their targets protecting them from attack by enemy fighters. Pilots loved it. It was heavily armed, stable, fast..., tough enough to bring them home again and again. In just a few months the P-51 had decimated the Luftwaffe and ruled the German skies. It made the job of our bomber pilots a bit easier and safer.

At the beginning of World War II few planes could fly more than 200 miles per hour. By war's end, late models of the P-51 could dash at 490 MPH in short bursts of speed.

When I saw him riding down our long curving lane on his bike I knew something big was up. We lived four or five miles apart and were together mostly at school and church or when our parents drove us for an occasional overnight at each other's home. Phil was intense and a bit winded from the long ride. "There was a crash last night. A bad one. Lets go see it," he spoke in a chatter of excitement. We rushed in to talk my mother into letting me go, and off we went on our bikes the three miles or so to the crash site.

It was near the end of the war, 1945 if memory serves well. It was a mild day, but overcast, misty, humid. It had rained heavily the night before. Phil and I had dreamed only of the excitement, of the glory of flight. We were little prepared for what we saw that morning standing at the edge of a quiet country road in Varina.

The Army Air Force called it the C-45. It was a beautiful, swift, twin-engine plane far ahead of it's time in speed and comfort. Built before World War II as the civilian Beechcraft DS-18, the "Twin Beech," it was pressed into military service in several different versions as a trainer, light cargo plane, and personnel carrier. There were four army men aboard, including the pilots, and one unfortunate navy man who had "hitched" a ride somewhere. Richmond's Byrd Field had become a temporary wartime Army Air Force base.

The plane left on that stormy night, developed engine trouble of some sort, turned back toward the runway, and arched in a shallow dive into a wet grassy little field next to a small family graveyard.

The high speed impact of the plane's nose and fuselage plowed a shallow trench in the grass and mud of the field, bounced the shattering pieces back into the air, spraying hundreds of bits and shards of metal and men into the forest. The tail of the plane with its dangling tail wheel and ten feet or so of flattened fuselage was tightly wrapped around a big tree twenty-five feet up it's trunk. The white nylon of someone's parachute was draped from another tree, torn open by the force of the crash, not because anyone had time to jump.

Awed and subdued, Phil and I said little to each other, quietly watching as somber men dressed in military fatigues carried things hidden in tarpaulins to waiting trucks. In wartime, with so many planes in the air, crashes were common around military bases. The tired men in work uniforms had been searching the forest since shortly after midnight. Little more than two hours after we arrived they completed the search, got in their trucks, and left the bits and pieces to anyone who wanted to pick through them.

Phil and I, walking warily under the tail section high in the tree, found the pilot's shattered instrument panel. It's dials and switches were torn asunder and streaked with blood and human tissue. The stopped instrument panel clock was one of those dials. The C-45, and the men on board, dove into the ground at 12:05 a.m.

When we were 14, in the last days before my family moved from Varina into the deep South, Phil and I made a pact with each other. We agreed, come what may, we'd have a reunion at the Hotel Richmond at the age of 21. We stayed in touch by letter for years. Soon after we left Phil wrote describing the carnage of an airliner crash near Byrd Field that made national headlines. I made two trips back to Varina in those years but missed seeing him both times.

After high school, for a while, Phil seemed to have more interest in driving farm tractors than flying. I hung around airports in Rome and Birmingham buying and bumming rides in many different planes, and spent two years in a high school Reserve Officers Training Corp. I fibbed about my age to join the Alabama Air National Guard at 16 so I could ride in some of the same warplanes Phil and I'd studied and dreamed about.

But then Phil's letter came saying that he'd joined the Air Force. In letters he spoke of his basic training and the base itself in the same glowing terms we'd always shared when we dreamed of flying. The last letter came with two pictures of himself and a lovely young woman named Nelda. From the words of that letter I had little doubt that, for Phil, she was the one.

Military pilots, of necessity and training, are supremely confident of their skill and vigorously tenacious in their aims. Wartime missions demand determination, even at the risk of life.

Peacetime should be a different thing. Missions turned foolhardy by worsening conditions can be aborted. Lives and multi-million dollar equipment can be spared to practice again at a more favorable time. Other than to the human ego, there's no need to fear loss in the more sensible course.

But then, when a very high ranking officer, a General or an Admiral, places himself in another officer's fighting machine his presence cannot help but upset the balance of options. A younger, lower ranking officer may feel inspired, driven to prove his mettle, to demonstrate his courage and skill and devotion to duty rather than choosing the safer course. If all ends well, the lower rank will have another thumbs-up on his record. The officer of high rank can only wonder about the silent pressure of his presence.

Twenty-one of the men aboard RB-36H #721 were designated as Crew H15 of the 718th Strategic Reconnaissance Squadron, a division of the 28th Strategic Reconnaissance Wing.

Captain Jacob H. Pruett, Jr. of Charlestown, West Virginia was pilot and aircraft commander. The co-pilot was Captain Orien F. Clark of Rapid City, SD.

Brigadier General Richard Elmer Ellsworth of Erie, PA, Wing Commander, and Major Frank C. Wright of Eagle, Idaho, his Chief of Wing Operational Planning, took over and flew long over-water portions of the 7 hour, 40 minute flight.

As weather grew worse and worse Captain Pruett took control of his plane. He knew it far better than his commanders.

The B-36 was built with six piston engines mounted backwards on the wings with propellers pushing the plane through the air. When the design was found to be underpowered four jet engines were added. They were hung in pods, two under the outer section of each wing.

When an engine fails the prudent flyer claws upward, if his remaining engines can give that saving grace. Altitude is his only chance to see, to look wider and farther, to choose, for time to think, to figure out what's wrong, what to do. But...even the failure of two of those jet engines in icing conditions failed to deter them from doggedly holding that dangerous altitude. They flew the last few hundred miles on instruments alone, two engines dead, completely blind, in steady sleet, freezing drizzle, and fog, leading 11 others behind them.

#721's navigator, Captain Harold G. Smith of Lyndhurst, NJ had factored headwinds and tail winds into his calculations. He was sure he'd direct the pilot, and the other planes, to climb 2,000 feet above the craggy North American coast before they reached land.

The four pilots and the navigator carefully reported their position every hour at planned points across hundreds of miles of ocean. They never knew that the awful weather had sabotaged one of their position reports and calculations. Instead of the 160 Knots of speed their instruments showed, they were actually moving at 202 Knots in a much stronger tailwind. They reached the coast far sooner than anyone expected.

Burgoyne, Newfoundland, in the 1950's, was a tiny fishing village on Random Island about 60 miles east of Gander. In the morning hours of March 18, 1953 people of the village listened helplessly as the giant plane rumbled past, just 1,000 feet overhead.

59

Exactly 7 hours and 40 minutes after lift-off from Lajes Field, with Captain Pruett flying at cruising speed, straight and level, still on instruments and completely blind, RB-36H #721 crashed into a low mountain in the frigid wilderness near Burgoyne Cove. A huge explosion and fireball woke villagers miles away.

Not in the cockpit, but far back in the plane, Airman Second Class Phillip T. Mancos, Jr, Gunner, rode to the end of his life that morning above the startled people of the tiny Newfoundland fishing village.

He was in that place, at that terrible moment, riding the big, beautiful, doomed silver bird ...because of the boyhood dream he and I shared during the years of World War II in the quiet countryside of Varina. Phil was only 21 years old.

In Varina, his father was told not to look because fire had partially reached him. But, like most fathers, Phillip T. Mancos, Sr. had to know that it was really his son they'd sent home. His father, his mother said, was never the same after that day. The hurt just never went away.

Riding with Phil to the awful end of that flight... were not only General Ellsworth, the three other pilots and the navigator, but SSgt Ira V. Beard of Sentinel, OK; 1Lt Clifford W. Bransdor of Chicago, IL; A2c Keith E. Hoppens of Harvard, NE; A1c Theodore J. Kuzik of West Orange, N.J.; Capt William P. Maher of Manchester, NH; TSgt Jack H. Maltzberger of Lake Stevens, WA; 1Lt Edwin J. Meader of Delaware, IA; Maj John T. Murray of Milwaukee, WI; A2c Robert H. Nall of Hattiesburg, MS; 1Lt James E. Pace of Tampa, FL; TSgt Walter A. Plonski of Scranton, PA; 1Lt James A. Powell, Jr. of Knoxville, TN; A2c Morris H. Rogers of Cleanfield, UT; Capt Stuart G. Tauhl of Bessemer, MI; SSgt Robert E. Ullom of Kingsville, TX; A1c Burse J. Vaughn of Evansville, IN; and Msgt Jack S. Winegardner of San Fransisco, CA.

Of the twelve giant aircraft which left Rapid City Air Force Base for the far reaches of the Atlantic, all but #721 made it home. But, it was only immense good fortune that saved those behind the leader.

It was not an officer who discovered their peril. That

fact of history takes nothing away from fine officers who flew the other giant planes and hundreds of airmen safely over thousands of miles of ocean. It speaks to the vital role the non-commissioned play in military missions.

Pilot, Captain Deane Curry, had just settled down for a nap. Co-pilot Captain Ira Purdy was flying when Master Sergeant Harold Parsley, a gunner in the second RB-36 just fifteen minutes behind #721, yelled over the intercom to the pilots on the flight deck of his huge bomber, "Are there supposed to be trees down there....?" He was wide awake, alert. Unlike the pilots, he'd had time for sleep during the long flight, and he was positioned to look down instead of straight ahead through the cockpit windscreen. It was his glance that found a tiny hole in the fog and clouds.

The pilots, shocked by his words, leaped to full attention, full-powered their RB-36 into straining, engine-screaming climb, barely skimming the trees and rocks of Newfoundland that loomed suddenly out of the fogbank. In their saving, they were given the chance to alert those behind them.

Hours later, unbelievably, another bomber, a B-29 sent to search for #721, crashed in the effort, killing all ten of her crewmen, too. It was the saddest of peacetime missions for the 28th Strategic Reconnaissance Wing.

Military bases are not named for soldiers of the rank and file...for young Privates or Sergeants or Airmen Second Class. That privilege is reserved for those who lead the way and, perhaps, that's the way it should be.

On June 13, 1953 our nation's Five-Star General and President, Dwight D. Eisenhower, along with South Dakota Governor Sigurd Anderson traveled to Rapid City Air Force Base to honor a member of the lost crew. Brigadier General Richard Elmer Ellsworth, was loved and respected by military and local people alike. On that day President Eisenhower changed the base's name to Ellsworth Air Force Base.

I wish Phil could have been there to see that ceremony. There were echelons of wide-winged B-36's on display, massed military men in parade formation, thousands

61

of Rapid City citizens, the Governor of South Dakota, the President of the United States. He would have been so proud, as I know he was proud to fly in the mighty B-36.

Phil's father, lived to his mid-seventies. His mother was 93 when last I saw her. She lived, still, in the house by the side of Richmond's rural route 5 where she and her husband guided their son to manhood.

The three of them were a strong, happy family when Phil and I were boys, but after the terrible morning in a tiny faraway fishing village there was a core of sadness that held fast. He was an only son, an only child. Long before, his mother had been a teacher at the Varina school where Phil and I shared our growing. It was years before she and her husband could bring themselves to take down the big, yellow airplane model, a Piper Cub, which Phil had built and hung from the ceiling of his room when he and I dreamed of flying.

As years gathered, far into the 1990's, there was an odd sense of the fullness of time when I sat with Lydia in her home, in Phil's home. It remained unchanged, ever yet as familiar as my own, with the same look and feel and scents of a time five decades past. It was always a fleeting glimpse back to beginning, of roots on which a life is built, while the open fields of Varina around it grew smaller, fewer.

The dark wood of an antique, upright piano had commanded the small living room from the time of our childhood. On it's top, with smaller family pictures and the sheet music of long ago, sat a silver framed 12x14 photograph of an ever-21 young man, his United States Air Force uniform proudly crisp, starched. The smile is kind, gentle... one his mother and I knew so well. It watched over that loved home for forty-four years after he was gone..., and now it watches over mine.

Through the creeping days of decades, I've wondered about the designs of life. When we were boys together it seemed that Phil was the stronger and steadier and smarter. And yet, I am the one who was given the gift of years...for learning and growing, for family and home and children, for the bittersweet tastes of failure and success, for gain and loss, rebounding to go on.

I've wondered why the feeling of friendship has stayed

so clear, close. When I've crept over mountains I thought I couldn't climb, found success where failure loomed, achieved when I felt unworthy...I've wondered another thing.

God, certainly, would never take everything from one, just to give to another. But, when the unexpected, the inexplicable, the unchangeable has come to pass...might He send a Guardian Angel?...a Guardian Angel who knows one's weaknesses and strengths and hopes and dreams better than any other of the heavenly host?

It was on Monday, January 27, 1997 that Phil's mother, Lydia Ellen Kovacs Mancos, passed from this life. She was laid to rest by the side of her husband and son in a place called Sunset not far from Richmond. Like so many mothers who have sent sons to war, Lydia shared the longing for a homecoming that could never be. After the terrible morning in Newfoundland, she lived long, long years with the faith and courage and strength and peace she taught her son.

I know, too, she spent that time in the hope of the grand old hymn of Varina's Laurel Hill Methodist Church ..."in the sweet bye and bye, we shall meet on that beautiful shore." Lydia Mancos was 95.

THE SPLENDOR OF OCTOBER!

IF THERE'S WEATHER in God's Heaven, it can only be October..., borrowed from the gentle, soothing fragrance of it's east wind.

We shudder at the prospect, but every now and then it might be rainy. In a rare year the brisk north wind of winter may creep in far too soon.

Most often, though, October on Northwest Florida's magnificent Emerald Coast is ...well...perfection!

Only then do Monarch butterflies, air-dancing, palette-splashes of lavish color, glory the shortening days as they flit through to the winter warmth of Mexico.

It's the cool crystal-blue sky we've longed for during the steamy summer months, sun that beams wonderful, dozing warmth instead of pressing heat, fresh crisp sea wind, quiet left by vacationers headed home.

For years it was a delight we kept to ourselves, a secret we were slow to share, time when we who love this sea-brushed sand can peer for miles down an empty, windswept beach, and know this land is ours.

And often the slower, sleepy, contented pace of October drifts on...through November, into December, almost to Christmas, before the brief chill of January and February.

Yet, even in the splendor of October, those who need high-arched hills and deep green valleys, and thin, weak mountain air will look away. Our curious land is as flat as the blue-emerald water of it's bays and sound and bayous, until twenty miles or so inland, it begins an oh-so-gentle undulation.

The peaks we see are seldom more than demure, sugar-white dunes guarding the last grip of shore. Treasured with golden sea oats and low, wind-twisted pine and scrub oak, they are as lovely to us as forests of stately long leaf yellow pine towering blue-sky tall a brief walk inland.

As years have convened, gathered, a few mini-metros have grown sprawling in our piney woods to lay bounty of the city at hand. Still, even in Pensacola and Fort Walton

Beach and Destin and Panama City and Tallahassee it's just a few minutes escape to the silence of field or forest or empty seaside.

It's not that we don't love the bikini summers on this magnificent beach. Truth is, every loved hearth has an annoyance or two which sons and daughters of the land suffer proudly. California has earthquakes and big forest fires and fog and sliding mud to carry homes away down hill. In America's mid-west, tornados slash the earth out of night-dark thunder storms. In Chicago's winter the lake wind is rapier sharp, and Buffalo's blizzard piles snow to the roof of cars.

In light of other's imperfections, we might concede that an Emerald Coast summer is often a steam bath of pressing heat and cloaking humidity, weighing us to pleasures of the slower "Southern" pace. Yet, to those whose roots go deep, it's just the familiar aura of home. Not so long ago it meant shaded porch swings, cardboard fans with popsicle-stick handles, cold Southern sweet tea, the clink of ice in fat, tall glasses, and the wonderful aroma of fried chicken drifting through open windows of a Sunday noon.

Few doubt the wonder of air conditioning that brought us chilled "nawthuners" and their silver...but, as sure as dimes shine, it cost us a part of ourselves.

Our brush with the subtropics brings us alligators. Far fewer, we're glad to say, than in South Florida. There's enough, though, to make us watchful in reedy flats on the shores of Santa Rosa Sound, and along rivers called Yellow, and Shoal, and Blackwater, and Perdido..., or near the banks of wee lakes nestled close to the sea.

We know to approach Palmetto clusters warily. They might be hideaways for deadly rattlesnakes, long as a tall man, thick as his arm.

In late summer and early Autumn a bold hurricane might stalk, threaten..., sometimes find us. Then our peaceful ocean's pulse can soar from whisper, from rhythmic thunder, to howling scream....rise on fearful sea-legs, hurl itself ashore like a million bellowing lancers on white steeds, madly charging a last lonely outpost.

Aahh, but then... there's October!

In quiet forests, along peaceful roads, doe and fawn, opossum, brown fox, the armor-plated armadillo are readying for the brief chill of our Emerald Coast winter.

Deeper in piney woods are turkeys and small brown bears and quail and bobcat and sometimes a Florida Panther.

At night big sea turtles plod the shore to nest their eggs. In brilliant sunshine white fiddler crabs rush, busy-legged, from beach hole to beach hole just ahead of the last foamy rush of ocean waves.

When the wind is up, sand as white as a maiden's glove blows and skitters in ankle low tumble-haze, drifting across blacktop roads by the sea.

You see..., east wind aims to be October's breezy, balmy breath. But when it's up, bustling, willful, it drives steep, choppy, bone-rattling little waves westward down the Bay.

None to soon, for our taste, it's a like breeze that welcomes Spring again. For January and February, even on the Emerald Coast, might flaunt bold, blasting, icy winds wandering from Northeast to North to blustery Nor'westers that shake a boat at it's pier like a rag in the teeth of a hound.

Long before October, when Spring has slipped away, it's the south wind, strong, steady, heavy with the salty scent of the sea, that bears the hot rush of summer onto Northwest Florida's Emerald Coast.

The Splendor of October could not be without her ocean, without the roar, the muted rhythm of murmuring surf, whispered to quiet forests and fields and small country towns little more than an hour away from a glistening beach.

The sea-mood rushes, drifts, in mutating seasons..., but October is it's heady time. Creeping in through ocean passes it surrounds us with salty fragrance and creatures of the deep. It's very essence melds cloistered waters, deep blue, emerald ringed, into a Bay ever-rippled by winds from the sea. In some long-ago it was named Choctawhatchee for Indian people who first cherished our land. And for those who bend sail to fresh breeze it is wave-washed perfection like October.

It's in October we'll sail from Smack Point, tacking hard for hours into the east wind, 'til we come hard about near Destin tired, exhilarated, content. The sail home is itself a breeze, October's wind behind us.

In gentle sunshine, fresh east winds, the big, golden harvest moon of October, we who share these piney woods and gleaming beaches find an uncommon equinox. In it's meandering hours there's the dream to fish and sail, to lie tanned and lazy on a lonely beach, to romance the night away near a bold, shimmering, silver moon-path on the sea.

Perhaps it might be to contemplate yesterday, the meaning our days have given us, what we might give to the hope of tomorrow.

It is surely time apart, space between, a slowing, nodding in the chair, a somnolent pause after steamy heat and hurry...until the lavish, bustling family seasons of Thanksgiving and Christmas, the uneasy chill that follows.

In October's warm-cool drowsiness, there's the other side of Spring fever, a world that seems lingering, easy...splendid, luxuriant days we wish could drift on and on...to a sunset far in the future.

Saunterin' with Lowenbrau

A FEW YEARS AGO...well, ok!...a lot of years ago...it would have meant a cool, frosty brew on a hot Northwest Florida summer afternoon. It wouldn't have meant one of those pricey imported ones, though. Not many, among the handful of us in the two-fisted, hard-drinkin' Fort Walton Beach of those years, had heard of them in the '50's. It wouldn't have been one of the now trendy "lite" beers, either. It would've been a hearty old Schlitz or Bud or Millers, the kind that makes the old guy who drinks too many look like he's hiding a watermelon under his shirt.

"Past-noon" sounds a bit younger than "sunset",doesn't it? Anyway, four decades after suds seemed cheering, in these easier-goin', "past-noon" years, saunterin' with Lowenbrau means something a lot different.

In her first family, there was a college-age son who somehow got to do the naming. So, when the little ones came along, there were Michelob and Budweiser and Schlitz. I think there may have been some others, but I've forgotten their alehouse names.

Lowenbrau was the littlest, the runt of the litter. Sandee, her adopted Momma these past fourteen years, says she was the cutest, the most adorable of all. Everyone she meets agrees. Her Momma says she's part Cock-a-poo and part Peek-a-poo, whatever that may add up to. The thing is, though, it takes a lot of time to explain why an adorable little eight pound pooch is named for a beer...so her Momma just calls her Lolo.

The years when I have more time than her Momma have crept up a lot sooner than expected. I guess that's why it's fallen my job to see that Lolo takes two long walks every day. Her Momma is ver-r-r-ry organized and scheduled with walks. God forbid a little doggie should get. . . well . . . constipated.

Come to think of it, Lolo's Momma is very organized and scheduled about a lot of things. She's very neat and fastidious, too. One can't leave un-neighborly "deposits" on

68

neighbor lawns. Every other doggie in Northwest Florida does it, but Lolo and I aren't allowed. We buy clear little plastic bags - like the one your newspaper comes in. They're just the right size to fit, almost to the elbow. Pick up the doggie-poo...your hand stays as clean as a spring rain! Turn it inside-out and...voila! Even when Lolo's Momma walks with us, I carry the doggie-poo. Sometimes, I wonder about that!

At first she made us carry extra little brown paper lunch bags so we could slip the plastic bags inside. It was a bother, so we quit doing it. Frankly, Lolo and I don't care whether anybody sees. It's a natural thing, isn't it? Sometimes, when we're waving to someone, we forget and wave the hand that's carrying the dogie-poo. Occasionally, I guess, that might be embarrassing when we're waving to the President of the Women's Garden Club or someone equally eminent. But, we don't worry about it. In a way we feel important, like big environmentalists or something. It's not likely our tidiness is doing much to save the Ozone layer, though.

It's a wonder just how independent and determined a little eight pound being can be. I like to walk full steam ahead, striding along at a healthy pace. In fact, my old friend and family sawbones, Dr. Roger D. Riggenbach, "matured" these twenty-five years right along with a lot of his patients, says the walks might be good for the rest of us, too.

Lolo, on the other hand, likes to saunter. For awhile she'll tippy-toe along as nice as you please, then suddenly she'll stop so fast I nearly run over her. She'll stand and look around and sniff. I can't figure out whether she needs to rest 'cause she's nearly my age in doggie years, or whether the Northwest Florida ocean wind smells as good to her as it does to me. Sometimes she just looks at me as if to say, "Ok, Bozo! What next?" But then - to tell the truth - when she's ready, she just heads off on whatever course she chooses without waiting for an answer.

It's amazing how hard a little eight pounds can pull. She wanders here, sniffs there,   checks this out, wets that....and that...and that...and that. Sometimes, I think her eight pounds must have a twenty-pound bladder.

And what an actor! She should get an Emmy,

pretending she's not limping when she gets a "stickey" in her foot. It's hard to blame her for trying to hide it. Northwest Florida sandspurs hurt like the dickens when we pull them out.

Going for a ride in the car is almost as exciting as going to see Gramma. How sweet it is - as Jackie Gleason used to say - to see wide smiles of approval from the windows of other cars when she stands and peers out the window of her Jeep Cherokee. Often, we're startled by wild snapping and snarling and bouncing in the other car's window, but it's not the driver. She still gives as good as she gets when somebody else's car-riding doggie questions her authority.

To be sure, Lolo hasn't a clue as to how small she really is. On the ground she'll charge to the end of her leash, yapping frantically, at the biggest of dogs. We've seen quite a few of them turn tail and run. It's the same with us, isn't it? It's not our size, it's how intent and determined we are that makes us winners.

Sometimes, saunterin' with Lowenbrau, I think about little friends who've shared these many years. It's hard to think of chickens as such, but there were thousands of them with us on the farm. The ducks were a lot more sociable. There was Midget, a little brown and white Fox Terrier. He chased cars. We buried him under the weeping willow tree in the back yard, next to the shop door. A big, white, nanny goat named Alice joined our family because brother Jeff was allergic to cow's milk when he was born. At the awkward age of thirteen, I had to learn - untutored - how to coax the milk from her. I was a country kid, but I'd never even milked a cow! April and Tonto, Alice's little ones, were born later. City kids can't imagine how much fun baby goats can be.

Later, in grown-up times, came Bourbon, a fluffy chow doggie, white as snow. In those wilder, woollier years of Fort Walton Beach, he licked the bottle on the way to a party. There was Stretch-A-Mile-Blue-Eyes, the Siamese cat who followed son James home. Caesar, the calico cat who turned out to be a lady, stayed with us for nineteen years until her time ran out. After we found out he was a she, it was too late to change her name. Gino was daughter Jill's pal for seventeen years. It's hard to picture a pooch more proud to

70

be at the business end of a leash. Muffin, daughter Dana's white Angora cat didn't last long because of a too-busy street, and her first Parakeet somehow found the only place he could get in trouble, the depths of the toilet bowl. Pedro, the other Parakeet, and a tiny Toy Poodle had to be given other homes because some of us were allergic. And, there was Lady, the little roly-poly black Chihuahua who looked after our mother and father, and the rest of us, for so many years.

It might seem a little nutty, but I've always talked to animals. Some think they can't understand. We can see how the sound of our voice affects them...comfort for pain, the soothing of fear, praise. Of course, the cowboy who talks to his horse and sings to calm the herd at night knows they understand. Forget the chickens. I know 'em like the back of my hand. They understand nothing but a tossed handful of corn. Ducks, at least, stare with seeming intelligence, watching our every move. I never could tell whether Alice or April or Tonto listened. To save our backsides, we learned rather quickly not to bend over in front of them. We talked to them, hugged them anyway.

It's our doggie friends who seem to learn language, to know individual words, to have a listening vocabulary. Horses learn a few commands and monkeys probably do best of all. Most of us never get the chance to test the understanding of those societies.

There's no doubt Lolo understands "go" and "treat" and "walk" and "Gramma" and "supper" and "Momma" and "car" and "ride" and "no". We see proof every day. Just as clearly, though, she's often torn between "no" and "I wanna..." She knows the word "here", but she ignores that one, too, when it suits her. The word "bath" sends her under a chair, and she does just as well with "ride" and "eat" and "hungry" and "leash", and of course she knows her name. Even a cat knows that, although she, or he, usually pretends not to. Any way, it's nice to think they understand. Sometimes, it helps to tell them things we don't want others to know.

Lolo is dancing, excited, waiting for the word "walk" by 6:00 a.m., and pretty impatient by the time she drags me out at 7:00. Our island way of life is as delightful to us as it is to her. The ocean is walking distance away. We can see the waterfront of Fort Walton Beach over river-like waters of Santa Rosa Sound that begin just across the street. Tugboats and big barges, and yachts, and sailboats, and jet skis go by. There's heat and humidity that reek of Florida, a lot of white sand, and green grass, and trees, the sound of ocean surf, the warm glow of sun, and a moon that seems to belong to us alone. Mostly there are quiet, sleepy, peaceful streets on which we wend our way. We might saunter past a couple of Alabama or Georgia vacationers on summer walks, and in winter, a few Canadians of the "past-noon" years. Often they stop to talk, and they all wish they were saunterin' with Lowenbrau.

We're lucky, it seems to me, if we have love in our lives. Our little friends often contribute much of that. But, there are other things vital to human well-being. Along with pride and happiness and self-respect and a feeling of success, we need humility to balance the tenor of our exis-tence.

When I think about that, when I feel too successful, get too full of myself....I find all the humility I need by recalling one thing. Remember those doggie deposits Lolo's Momma thinks aren't "neighborly" to those who live down the street?

Well.....I carry 'em home!

A Glance Toward "Hail"

Tallahassee's Leon County also bears his name. Northwest Florida's diminutive, somnolent, pervasively rural Ponce de Leon is far different. Seldom has it yearned for the opulence gathered by Florida's capital city, nor even the fame unearthed by the state's Spanish explorer. To be sure, the lovely running spring he found there is a modest fame of sorts with it's Interstate 10 exit marker. But then, it is hardly the Fountain of Youth Ponce de Leon himself sought.

Those born in Ponce de Leon, ten miles or so from DeFuniak Springs, are inured to the quiet fields and forests and smattering of neighbors. The few who come there seem to seek that solitude.

And too, perhaps, many need a place where starting over again with little is a mingling of like souls, a token of hardiness rather than oddity, or shame. That, it seems likely, is what brought him, for he, his wife, and baby were little known, little noticed in Ponce de Leon before that awful morning. His only other relative appeared to be a daughter, offspring of a previous marriage. She was already wed at the age of eighteen, a time in life which can sometimes be artless, unruly. There was only one who claimed to be his friend. He lived miles away, without a telephone.

There must have been a settlement of sorts from some disabling work injury. He'd recently bought more pricey things, some hunting guns and a four wheel trail rider.

Certainly, among his meager possessions was a video recording camera, for he wielded it in desperation, in hope of revelation to some wider world.

It is this belonging that flickers on. First a black screen with lightning-like zig-zags, then suddenly clear eyed, in full color, looking into a small, unpretentious living room. At the fore is a sofa, clearly long used. It's fabric is of audacious plaid, so like those in the homes of millions of American workers.

The room seems cared for, though a bit disordered. Still, the painful feel of poorness, of hard times, is inescapable. The camera pans down to the carpet, to piles of pill bottles, to boxes with more pill bottles spilling out of them. It is clear at once they are prescription medications, not illegal drugs. The lens stares at this pile of trouble, maybe a bit too long, waiting until the pain sinks in, reaches out.

A looming shadow brushes past the camera, overwhelms the scene..., focuses into the form of a man of rather youngish middle age. He is much like the room itself, the same feeling of poorness, of hard times.

Sitting down on the threadbare sofa, he looks squarely, steadily into the camera. He shows not the slightest sign of being drunk, nor high on drugs. There is just the awful, intent sadness about him, a sense of deep, bottomless, dismaying despair. His face is calm, far too calm, deadpan, politely firm, terribly resolute.

"My name...," he speaks barely above a whisper, "...is Billy Ray Grimes." He wears dark work pants, a plaid shirt, a cardigan sweater. Even in the house, in front of the camera, there is the long billed work cap, so like millions of others.

He seems to remember the courtesy after he begins to speak, takes the cap off, placing it on the sofa beside him. His hair is curly, almost to his shoulders, long un-barbered.

"This is..." he says, and there's no way to escape the chill of the words, the level, determined, penetrating fullness of his eyes, "...my last will and testament...!"

The video records the exact time, 3:39 a.m. It gathers, hoards, in small glowing numbers on the TV screen, evanescent moments of life..., one precious minute at a time.

"I don't want to take my own life." The words are cool, matter of fact. Somewhere in his past there must have been the seasoning of God's order, of His Commandments. "I know I'm going to hell for what I'm about to do." In the working dialect of America's rural South, the word sounds like "hail."

For 44 minutes he clings to this chance to tell the world...someone ... anyone...about his plight.

"Before," he says, "I could work..., hold my head up high." It is of severely limited income that he speaks... long, intently, ruefully..., of rent due, phone bills, water bills, lawyers, of constant pain, debts owed to doctors, drug stores, at rambling length of family troubles that so often conflict the lives of disabled workers.

In that gently spoken account of torment there was much he didn't say. He may not have known, or not fully grasped, the politically driven rapacity that so often ravages support for those disabled by on-the-job injuries. Or perhaps, in those stark moments, he'd simply been pressed far beyond such understanding.

For generations, employers simply fired those disabled by on-the-job injuries, dumping them without family income, nor even medical care for the injury itself. As more humane, government-of-the-people became empowered in America, new laws compelled employers to provide for workers injured by the "bosses" machines or management failure. Worker Compensation insurance systems, under Federal and State law, were set up in virtually every state. Programs funded, not by taxes, but by private insurance premiums claim to assure American workers that on-the-job-injuries will not destroy their hope for a decent life.

And yet, in the majority of states, as big-business "conservatives" gain legislative power, that claim grows more empty with every legislative session. As a result poverty, bankruptcy, loss of homes, autos, and personal possessions, despair, depression and hopelessness are everyday calamities for far too many disabled workers and their families.

This is the reason why senseless acts of desperation..., impulsive, clumsy hold-ups, burglaries, thefts, family conflict, even suicides, are a recognized concern among medical professionals who treat America's disabled and unemployed. In fact, a December 1999 report published by the New England Journal of Medicine lists unemployment, following alcohol and drug abuse, as a leading cause of domestic violence.

In our modern work-a-day world, worker injuries and disabilities repeatedly result from violations by "the boss" of federal and state laws. Thousands of work place safety violations exposed annually by OSHA, the Federal Occupational Safety and Health Administration, clearly bear this out. It is recognized more and more that the increasing devastation of American workers disabled by their boss's machines or management practices today is a result of cozy, self-serving, politics between big insurance companies and politicians who favor big business far more than working citizens.

In the State of Florida for example, a "Republican revolution" taking hold in 1994 has wedded a Republican Governor, reportedly aligned with insurance companies, and a Republican controlled legislature. They seem to be maneuvering hard behind the scenes to warp legal protections, further damning the fate of disabled workers.

In this corporate-toadying environment, worker disability statutes, year by year, slant direly in favor of wealthy insurance companies. Their profits are rising rapidly, leaving far more families of disabled in distress. Disability insurance companies are now the most powerful of political wheeler-dealers. Chief among them is a huge, heavy-handed, firm which began as a modest association of Florida restaurant and hotels who chose to band together to fund their own disability insurance costs.

Florida's Governor, brother and son of American presidents, has booted at least four disability Judges out of office after disability insurance companies, or lawyers, sent secret letters to the Governor accusing the Judges, of "bias" against insurers, and "favoring" disabled workers.

The Governor fired them even though the Judges had undergone extensive review by Florida's State-wide Nominating Committee which unanimously approved their reappointment.

76

In Florida, juries are not permitted in disability cases. Judges, therefore, act fully as juries. The firing of Judges under those conditions is so intimidating it is equated to jury tampering by Florida legal insiders. Jury tampering - in any other venue - is considered a crime which would send an ordinary American citizen to jail.

In Florida's 2000 election furor, Appellate Judges who ruled in favor of Democratic candidate Al Gore were widely accused of partisan politics. Truth, more likely - as Judges and attorneys throughout Florida express dismay over what seems gubernatorial abuse of Florida's disability judiciary - is that the Appellate Court's rulings were driven by a hope to ensure judicial fairness at the Presidential level, aspiring that fairness might somehow be restored in Florida's court system.

In the Republican re-drawing of worker disability laws, insurers promised business leaders that changes in the law would bring reduced insurance costs. To the contrary, according to attorneys, settlements to repair the lives of Florida's disabled workers have been slashed up to 90%, skyrocketing insurance company profits, while insurance premiums paid by employers have remained the same or climbed even higher.

Under the administration of our two-term Republican Governor and Florida's Republican Legislature, payments to disabled workers are often up to a week or more late, making it agonizing for those disabled by their boss's machines or systems to provide even food for their families.

More grievous are legal insider hints that Republicans and their insurance company backers feel confident that Florida's growing flood of Black and Hispanic blue-collar workers won't be smart enough, or politically pro-active enough, to confront the political deal-making which promises to destroy disabled workers hope for a decent future.

"Privacy" laws claiming to protect "worker's personal information," severely hamper the public and media from gaining access to individual case facts. Therefore, damaging effects of changes to Florida's Workmens Comp laws are routinely hidden from public view.

Why...? Why would a clearly decent, affable, popular man conduct his Governorship in a manner so damaging to working Americans? The reason, it seems, may well be as simple as political funding.

If whispers in Tallahassee are faithful, the insurance companies, their clients, and hired lawyers sent $10,000,000 to the Governor's first election campaign. That one huge, leading, firm brags on an internet web site of it's wide spread political funding to members of Florida's House and Senate.

The result seems to be that Florida's insurers are now routinely able to deny legally required medical care at will despite the "law," run late with family disability payments, and use legal tactics to block court action for years at a time, stalling and stalling and stalling the legal determination of disability status and the financial shelter it gives.

Even worse, the Governor and Republican legislators seem to be pushing hard to deny injured workers the assistance of a fee-paid attorney, which would put total control of disability resolution in the hands of wealthy insurance companies.

There is, of course, no excuse a civilized society can accept for family violence, nor lessor illicit acts, even if impulsively driven by material need.

Doesn't it make sense, many ask, that those who claim to be "compassionate conservatives" should work to prevent family disaster through honest, truly workable programs that safeguard life for American workers disabled through injury caused by, or for, their employers?

He'd set no hampering of time, seeming just to need to talk it out until he was empty. As ticking minutes on the TV screen near 44, he seems to reach that emptiness.

There is a long, quiet pause, void at last of the anguish he yearns to leave with someone, some of us, some wider part of this world. In that hush, his eyes remain cool, calm, leveled directly into those of the camera.

"I had to do something," he asserts at last, quietly. "I just can't take it no more." For a moment or two he remembers, with words of gratitude, doctors who helped with free drug samples. He does not remember to praise them by name. His voice trails off into another long, level-eyed, unmoving quiet.

"I just can't leave my wife and baby alone," he says finally, stirring. "I don't want them to go through the hell I've been through anymore."

It is clear now..., frightening..., why his voice has been near a whisper, why the video has been played again and again and again to come to some understanding of his words. They are sleeping. He doesn't want to awaken them.

"I hope," he whispers, "I'll have the courage. For my own end of it."

He is silent again..., utterly still, gazing steadily into the eyes of the camera for a long, long moment, as though wondering if everything has been said..., perhaps hesitant, reluctant now.

It is 4:23 a.m. when he stirs, rises resolutely to his feet.

"I'd better get on with it...," he says finally, standing now. "...With what I've got to do."

His form looms large again as he moves toward the camera, brushes past it, clicking it off. The screen is black, flickering once more... cloaking the awfulness that is about to happen.

At 5:11 a.m. deputies reach the house, responding to his own 911 call. In his mailbox they find this video tape... just as he vowed.

Inside the small home were the bodies of Billy Ray Grimes 50, his wife Brenda Lee Kelly Grimes 38, and their 8 month old baby Crystal Odelia Dianne Grimes. They were all dead of shotgun blasts.

To be sure, there was an investigation of sorts by Walton County Deputy Sheriffs. It was half-hearted, at best. There seemed no question that Grimes and his family were struggling to get by on disability payments from some on-the-job injury. There was a hint, perhaps, that the injury might even have occurred in some other jurisdiction.

79

The point is, they just never bothered to find out what agency was responsible for his case, what might have been done to prevent this awful tragedy, nor others like it in the future. After all, they had their "perp." But, he was far beyond any meaningful reach of "the law" by then. Early on, deputies promised news reporters they'd find out the reason for this terrible crime.

Apparently, like far too many official inquiries into puzzling anti-societal acts driven by work disabilities, they decided after the reporters left it was too much trouble.

THEY CALLED 'EM
RETIRED COLONELS!

It was a while before I fully understood that they dreaded far more than the one lone rank. Truth was, abhorrent to the military caste, they lumped them all together. Retired officers of every ending, Lieutenant, Captain, Major, Colonel, General, even high ranking Civil Service execs, were parodied as 'Retired Colonels' by early Emerald Coast business leaders.

In unmistakable contrast to the fear of retirees, it could not have been more clear that we all profoundly revered our active-duty military compatriots.

Moreover, in my own span of growing, the dream to fly had caught fire, along with an awe of those who lived that exhilarating adventure. So, in the mid-1950's as I matured into management and civic affairs...to the point in business leadership where one might know such things...it was astonishing to hear puzzling grumbles of anxiety about our growing deluge of military "retirees."

To be sure, though, at virtually every business gathering of the founding years I knew, the caution, the deep trepidation, the fear, would somehow be shared. It was phobia that erupted rarely from a podium. Most often it was parsed in muted, personal discussions before or after the formality of a meeting.

"To save our business community...," I heard it said again and again, "...local people who love our area must, somehow..., someway..., delay those 'Retired Colonels' from overwhelming us, from gaining control of local civic plans and affairs...as long as possible!"

They knew it was coming, though. We were unveiling the most delightful seaside lifestyle in America, and it was obvious that more and more of the retirees purposefully aimed their last few active duty years toward Eglin Air Force Base, it's luxurious benefits, and our delightful Emerald Coast.

'Retired Colonels', pondered community leaders, were long isolated from, and seemed to have little grasp of working America. Still youthful, well heeled financially, they seemed braced with aggressiveness anchored to 20 years of "firing line" leadership.

They came with, it was surmised, no real remaining link to, understanding of, or concern for our Nation's business community, the driving force of America's free enterprise system.

Emerald Coast founders had observed another thing. Of far greater dread to working Americans, the 'Retired Colonels' came with an established reputation for opposing, criticizing, disputing, ravaging the business community in every area where they retired en masse.

They would assault the local business climate, it was muttered, with little more than personal selfishness in mind, a craving to get everyone else out of the way of their own luxurious retirement, linked to an utter lack of concern for others that seemed a natural order of military leadership.

In other words, how could those trained to kill-or-be-killed, to willfully send boys out to suffer the same fate, truly retain a sense of caring and respect for others, or respect the financial well being of American businesses and working families?

A thread of rank-happy, macho arrogance, drunkenness, adultery, seduced and abandoned women, unmarried pregnancies, neglected and abused families, and the midnight "requisitions" of government gear in which military bases seemed to wantonly wallow only served to sharply reinforce those fears.

On the other hand, pensioners from the not-so-lofty, non-commissioned, working ranks were a bit less doubted. They seemed more like us, better able to remember the importance of commerce, of America's free enterprise system, and the jobs it provides. More to the point, with their lower retirement incomes, they needed those jobs.

They were, indeed, working Americans...the early businessfolk who labored, loved, invested, risked what little they had to build this magnificent 'Playground Area' seaside we now smugly call the Emerald Coast. I knew them, and their hearts, personally and well.

There was never a doubt of their intense pride in "our" Eglin Air Force Base and the men and women who've staffed it over this half century. Those who proudly, and morally, wear the uniform have always been seen as heroes on our Emerald Coast. There might be an uneasy hint or two that some seemed reluctant, pledged more to lifelong guarantee and easy abundance rather than truly clinging to the warrior's calling.

Norfolk had signs that jeered, "dogs and sailors keep off the lawn." Many, if not most, military towns dealt just as disdainfully with the riotous, debauched, lecherous behavior framing the mood around "camps."

Emerald Coast businessmen had served their own military time, not in the extravagance of peace, but in the terrible straits of the Big War. With understanding born of personal experience they worked tirelessly, faithfully, on our Emerald Coast to craft the best rapport in America with Eglin's Air Force men and women who shared our lives for a while.

They kept the faith through thousands of wonderful friendships that could last little more than a year or so because of the military's penchant to transfer, transfer, transfer.

They kept the faith through spectacles of drunkenness, womanizing, brawling, and broken families.

They kept the faith when unit commanders hurriedly transferred troops arrested for criminal acts, out of the reach of Okaloosa County justice.

They kept the faith while Eglin leaders ran training classes teaching that all local business people were crooks, "out to rip off" military personnel.

They kept the faith while 'Retired Colonels' derided local citizens as "dumb rednecks" and "good old boys."

They kept the faith, painfully, while well heeled warriors and their wives sneered at our growing little towns, and small shops, and few restaurants, scornfully comparing us to New York and Chicago, London, Paris, Rome, Tokyo.

And they kept that faith, warmth, welcome, certain in their hearts that when the 'Retired Colonels' overtook us, Emerald Coast businessmen and women would be in for the fight of our lives to protect the real America...our local business economy, the jobs it provides to working Americans, and the flood of taxes it pays for government grandeur.

In the year 2003, five decades or so have slipped away since those fears first came to ear. Our magnificent Emerald Coast is, indeed, now resplendent with our 'retiree' compatriots. It is virtually impossible to find a family without at least one. Our neighborhoods, churches, schools, civic groups, are replete with them, multitudes who have become dear friends, often members of our own families. We have known so many who are kind and cooperative and giving, those who have been able to regain, after retirement, an understanding of what America is really all about..., even join profitably, eagerly, into our business community.

In that same, long, 50-odd span of years most of our Emerald Coast founders have slipped away, leaving few of us to remember, to weigh fear in the balance of time, and reality, and hard seasoning. As years amassed, one upon another, our dwindling Emerald Coast founders, though..., civil, caring, welcoming, respectful to the end, quietly noted fearful validation of their decades old dread of 'Retired Colonels.'

In the early '50's Valparaiso was the largest, the most visible of cities in South Okaloosa County. Right at the Eglin gate, it's future looked brightest of all. For decades, though, it's elected officials have been piloted by high ranking Eglin civil service executives, miles of it's pricey waterfront owned by military officers.

Valparaiso, in the year 2003, is now economically a dying little village, South Okaloosa County's smallest. It has virtually no industry, no interest in industrial development, a handful of marginal, fading little shops, few jobs and almost no substantial career opportunities for our children. It's big bank exists mainly on billions of America's tax dollars raked in from huge salaries on adjacent Eglin Air Force Base.

Thirty-five miles west, the town of Gulf Breeze, rigidly controlled for decades by high-ranked officers from Pensacola's Naval Air Station, has followed a like anti-business path to economic desolation. Gulf Breeze, in effect, is also a dying city devoid of industry, with little interest in industrial development, only a token handful of small, fading, service businesses, few jobs, and scant opportunity for worthwhile career development. For decades, it's local claim to fame has been a reputation as a police speed trap, it's city coffers heavily funded by unsuspecting travelers blue-lighted by traffic cops on main street, profitably aimed straight through town as U.S. Highway 98.

Pensacola Beach, linked to Gulf Breeze by a short bridge, and long controlled by the same Naval Officer class, Is the shabbiest beach resort area on the Emerald Coast. With Northwest Florida's largest city just a few minutes away it should be the largest and brightest, but 'Retired Colonels' rant, rave, and combat development at every turn. Comparably tiny Destin looks like a luxurious French Riviera compared to the aged run-down shacks, tattered little motels, and ragged "lawns" that haunt Pensacola Beach. The Navy 'Retired Colonels' seem avidly opposed to any meaningful development, tourists, or traffic that gets in the way of luxurious retirement. And they seem to care nothing for what may happen to working Americans who still need to earn an honest living for their families, provide jobs, make their businesses successful.

Across Santa Rosa Sound from Fort Walton Beach, the homeowners association of Okaloosa Island has, for well over two decades, seemed merely an extension of the Retired Officers Association. In the early 1960's, the Island was purposefully, wisely, divided into entirely separate commercial and residential areas in order to protect the needs of individual homeowners.

'Retired Colonels' though, who live on the high-priced residential side, have constantly attacked business folk who legally and properly developed the commercial side with tourist hotels and condominiums. It seems the 'Retired Colonels' have used every ruse to interfere with development, filing complaints of "building violations," rabidly opposing building permits, needed renovations, and loudly criticizing "those greedy businessmen" at every turn.

Most restaurants and shops have deserted Okaloosa Island leaving it near barren of services needed by residents. The situation has become so bad that the businessmen and women of Okaloosa Island recently tried to rejoin the 'real

America' by naming Okaloosa Island "Destin West," to the immense embarrassment of adjacent Fort Walton Beach. Destin is more than six miles away.

Okaloosa Island 'Retired Colonels,' through the Island Homeowner's Association, bitterly opposed - and forced removal of - a shield that would prevent death, injury, and property damage from falling objects at a new hi-rise condo. An innocent mistake made condo owners vulnerable to spite. They believed additional permitting unnecessary since the shield was tied on both sides to areas that were already fully, legally permitted. Self-centered retirees don't seem to care that death, injury, or property damage will very likely occur because of a hateful anti-business mind set.

Across the short span of Brooks Bridge from Okaloosa Island, city fathers have long, and wisely, planned redevelopment in downtown Fort Walton Beach. Modernization is sorely needed. Fort Walton Beach mushroomed from a tiny frame-building town of 2,388 souls in 1950, to more than 22,000 today, with little change in the heart of downtown.

Local citizens on City Council, dedicated working Americans, have labored tirelessly because they know that any city, especially in such a promising area as our Emerald Coast, benefits greatly from a beautiful, efficient city center.

But, for twenty years 'Retired Colonels' have fought viciously at every turn to interfere with down-town renovation in Fort Walton Beach. "Just bulldoze the G**Damn place down and build a park," they bugle. They don't care, it seems, that local citizens, working Americans who built our Emerald Coast, love the city and it's history.

In blissfully brief 20 year military 'careers', and for the rest of earthly days..., that's how it works ..., everything is government owned, a government handout.

As a result of 'Retired Colonels' vicious opposition to everything but their own welfare, and as seating of 'Retired Colonels' on the City Council burgeons, Fort Walton Beach sags toward the rank of a dying city, while Destin evolves as an astonishing economic wonder, America's new 'Riviera.'

City Council members have worked just as long to route U.S. Highway 98 traffic around Main Street. Every flourishing city in America has done so. It makes good economic sense, enhances traffic flow, sharply reduces the risk of accident, and eases the way for travelers.

Clear thinking local citizens, working Americans, are horrified that 'Retired Colonels' have stalled this prudent effort for two decades. Retirees continue to rail against it, tooth and nail, determined to force 50 to 60 mph highway traffic right through the congested central business district of Fort Walton Beach. They don't seem to care that it is a cruel, heartless risk to human life, and a monstrous barrier to the success of working Americans and their businesses. They howl that redeveloping downtown is an 'unfair tax' expense to other areas of the city.

Early Emerald Coast leaders grumbled that 'Retired Colonels, far more than other wealthy special interest groups in America, hated paying taxes simply because they were accustomed to the government paying for everything in their lives.

Truth is, though, that downtown renovation in this area of beautiful waterfront property will far more than pay for itself if done sensibly by knowledgeable, working Americans in the business community.

Threatening with a swinging axe, one couple mounted a standoff against city workmen, ranting and raving against the cutting of one lone tree. Removal of the tree was vital to the construction of utility services in that highly upscale area of Fort Walton Beach. Our Emerald Coast is centered in an intensely rural region. Likely, there are a hundred million trees in a radius of 25 miles. They grow heavily in the city itself. There is far...far... from a shortage of trees.

Liberated, though, from financial reality by highly brief careers, wondrous, never ending, taxpayer paid salaries, pensions, and benefits, makes it easy to regard one tree as more important than the needs of others, business success, jobs vital to working Americans.

Saving, expanding, and moving Eglin's, small, virtually unknown Air Force Armament Museum was solidly supported and partially funded by Emerald Coast business men and women. Oddly, many 'Retired Colonels' ranted, raved, and fought savagely against their own Air Force Museum. Why?

The new, expanded, and highly successful location is off-base and accessible to working American vacationers, a group loathed by many vociferous retirees because of the added traffic they might bring.

The Fort Walton Beach City Council began legislative efforts to shut down nude dance bars within the City because of severe problems with extreme noise, robberies, thefts, rape, mugging, assaults, and even murder.

Opposition by 'Retired Colonels' was savage. "Of course, I don't go in those places myself," wailed letters to the editor, "but if I wanted to, it's my right...and those nude bars should be allowed to operate."

That, as early Emerald Coast business leaders noted, is the atmosphere around every military base, the aura in which military people live for their 20 year careers. But, lest you think every one fits the same mold, it was a 'Retired Colonel', a good friend and fellow City Council member, who led the fight to rid Fort Walton Beach of nude bars.

It is 14 miles in either direction from Fort Walton Beach's Brooks Bridge to any other. All U.S. Highway 98 and Fort Walton Beach traffic to the beaches and the burgeoning City of Destin cram onto that one bridge.

Business leaders have long planned a second bridge to Okaloosa Island for convenience and hurricane safety of Island residents as well as thousands of hotel and condo guests. The west side of downtown Fort Walton Beach would be four minutes away instead of an eight mile round trip.

'Retired Colonels' who live on the high-priced side of the Island have fought savagely against the bridge, panicked that it might bring an extra car or two to the Island. The question is fair and resonant. Is luxurious retirement, devoid of bothersome, working, Americans more important than the convenience and safety of others? Early Emerald Coast leaders regarded that attitude as merely a continuation of the haughty wealth and class separation normal to military life, scorning lower paid ranks who will be ordered to risk death in combat.

Emerald Coast business leaders always knew Eglin and Hurlburt Air Force bases and their vital economic impact could be lost on the turn of a vote in Washington.

For that worrisome reason early businessmen and women worked tirelessly to expand our tiny vacation industry. Over years many organizations served that vital need. Our highly successful Tourist Development Council was set up by Florida's Legislature, funded not by local taxes but by vacationers themselves. Our Emerald Coast economy is far more stable, since tourism now looms even larger than the military segment of our economy.

Yet, it seems 'Retired Colonels' rage shrilly against our TDC at every turn, recently launching a vicious campaign to vote it out of existence. Why? To a number of strident retirees, tourists seem clearly to be nothing more than an annoyance intruding on luxurious retirement.

Were the fears of Emerald Coast founders real? Do far too many of those dreaded 'Retired Colonels' not care a whit about business owners, employees, families, working Americans who depend on tourism for jobs, food, clothing, and the simplest essentials of life?

For more than 50 years, local business citizens, working Americans, have fought tirelessly to find funding to build a Convention Center. With the guidance of Florida's Legislature and our local TDC, that goal is finally within reach.

For one thing, it is sorely needed as our main hope to have a suitable place to stage large local events.

In our bid for convention business, it's purpose never was to seek conventioneers during the main tourist season, increasing already heavy summer traffic. Truth is there's no place to house conventioneers then. Motels and condos are filled with vacationers. The logical, sensible idea is to enhance the industry by bringing in conventions during our slack fall, winter and spring seasons when so many employees are laid off, barely existing on unemployment checks until the next season.

Certainly not all, but far more than a few, of our 'Retired Colonel' friends have mounted the most vicious of attacks against local working Americans and our age-old need for a Convention Center.

Hatred of "tourists" seems thinly veiled by strident, slashing, criticism of the Convention Center itself..., it's location, it's design, it's cost, the streets leading to it, oddly even the wonderful fact that it will cost little in local taxes.

One old-time Emerald Coast founder put it this way. "It's not enough to be a hero. We can only be real Americans when we understand and support the heart of America, the capitalist economy that provides the core of all jobs and government taxes."

Not long ago, the age old dread of 'Retired Colonels' surfaced again in a quiet chat with an elderly friend. As a local business owner, he'd worked tirelessly for many years to further fine relations with our military compatriots, contributing mightily to the founding the Emerald Coast we know today.

"I guess we've learned a lot about them," I said.

"How so?," he wondered.

"Seems there really are some who're able to understand what America is all about, and join with local citizens in bolstering a robust business economy."

"Yes, that's been a pleasant, unexpected surprise," he mused. "Still, far too many of 'em viciously fight our business community at every turn. Their awful anti-business attitude has been devastating to Fort Walton Beach...let Destin leap far ahead."

"Painful to say...but, hard to deny...!"

"It's really sad isn't it...," he murmured quietly.

"Sad...?"

"Yeah...sad...! Sad that so many of our 'Retired Colonel' friends...folks who give so much to America ...and take a lot from America seem, well, uh...a bit un-American, ...even dangerous to America, in long, luxurious retirement years."

Dawn At The
Indian Mound Saloon

It was not that the Indian Mound Saloon wasn't profoundly a part of us in daytime, In fact, Bill William's little fishhead bar was a major presence on Main Street when that part of town was nearly all of Fort Walton Beach.

The building was smallish, perched right on the edge of the sidewalk in front of the ancient, earthen, Indian Mound itself. It seemed a bit unsteady, infirm with years. Inside was small, dim, wood paneled, with an old oiled wood floor that sagged and creaked uneasily underfoot. But Bill kept it's stucco facade freshly white-washed, starkly bright, gleaming in brilliance of our Northwest Florida sun.

A huge sign seemed to overwhelm the little place, standing wide, tall, far above the black tar roof. High in the air, it's top ballooned into a far wider circle proudly bearing the face of an Indian chief in full, splendid, feather head-dress. Neon tubes framed the sign, top to bottom, around the face of the Indian chief, glowing bright red in sullenness of night through palm trees that lined the sidewalks.

Truth was, the sign said "Indian Mound Bar." That was the name Bill Williams awarded long before Claude Jenkins tagged it "The Best Damned Saloon On The Miracle Strip," and made it late-night famous among our "beautiful people" of those years. But then, I've told you about that in Claude's tale, "The Best Damn Writer On The Emerald Coast," so I won't belabor it.

Bill Williams seemed an old man to my youthfulness then, perhaps though, only in his late fifties or early sixties. He was an influential personage, well known to all of us, quietly, sensibly spoken...at some earlier time a Fort Walton Beach City Councilman.

Moreover, he was a pleasant looking man, likely handsome in younger years, with deeply tanned face so prosaic to old-timers of the Emerald Coast. Day or night, I never saw him without the small bar glass, half full of amber

91

whiskey, sipping along... but I never saw him drunk. He managed to abide that way until he was 84, always well liked, deeply respected. I clearly recall the flood of tears on the cheeks of his long-time bar maid the day of his funeral.

Like most of the early Fort Walton Beach business and civic leaders, Bill Williams had spent his time in the Big War. He didn't talk about it. None of them did. It was not to risk their lives for big salaries, or short careers, or pensions, or life long benefits that they went. It was to save their country...and for a mere 21 bucks a month or so. Then, if they were lucky, to come back home and go to work.

Bill did maintain an unspoken part of World War II, though. Behind the bar of the Indian Mound Saloon, around the edges of the big back bar mirror, over the double row of colorful, backlighted, whiskey bottles were mementos of that conflict .... helmets, hand grenades, bullets, weapons, shoulder patches. There was a world of it, cramming the edges of the mirror, even attached to the ceiling. I never asked whether he brought all of it back from the war himself, or whether his customers saw the display, added to it. The thing is, those were not mementos of our Eglin Air Force Base. They were of the Army, the mud slogging foot soldier.

During the day, the Indian Mound Saloon was a sleepy, slow moving little bar. A few regular patrons drifted in and out, daytime imbibers who drank not because they were party goers, but because they had to. At the end of the day, there'd be the meager rush of after-work boys dropping in for a beer or two before heading home for supper. In the early evening, again, would be the trickle of regular bar patrons, mostly blue collar folk and fishermen of those years.

At 2:00 a.m. the fancy places like Docie Bass' Rep Room Lounge at Staff's Restaurant, Bishop's Bar & Lounge, Jim Miller's Flamingo Bar & Lounge, the Magnolia Club, Chuck Clary's Bayview Lounge & Supper Club, the Spanish Villa Night Club, Paul Robert's fledgling Seagull Restaurant & Bar, Julius Miller's Ocean City Cocktail Lounge, and far down the beach, Docie Bass' Spyglass Inn, closed for the night.

It was then that Bill William's little fishhead bar came alive... a rendezvous for "beautiful people" from the more luxurious watering holes who were still rollicking in a party mood, determined to party 'til dawn. Following the lead of swashbuckling, hard guzzling, carousing, military pilots, Fort Walton Beach was equally a partying, hard drinking town in that era.

In 1958, there were two more who shared the Indian Mound Saloon's late night rendezvous, at least on Monday nights. My boss, advertising and circulation manager of the Playground News, and I were far from party goers. We were of the callow after-work patron class, at least that day of the week. The difference was, our workday on Mondays at the paper stretched from 8:00 a.m. in the morning to 2:00 or 3:00 a.m. deep in the night.

The Playground News was printed on the presses of the Pensacola News Journal. Their courier picked up our ad layouts and typed news copy at 1:00 a.m. After that, for an hour or two, the ad manager had to "dummy" the pages... positioning all ads in a specified ratio on each page to let Editor/Publisher Wayne Bell know how many columns of space he had to fill with news.

So, at 2:00 or 3:00 in the morning, exhausted and hungry, we'd stumble in to the Indian Mound Saloon for a beer or two and perhaps a couple of purple hen-fruit fished out of the gallon jar of pickled eggs on the mahogany bar.

Dawn comes early in Northwest Florida's summer. A couple of beers, a few purple eggs, a bit of parley with rousing, inebriated friends and we'd be staring the early light of a new day in the face when we headed out the door of the Indian Mound Saloon for home and a bit of sleep.

On that particular Monday night she was there. A "tourist" sticks out like a Greyhound bus on a back woods road in a tiny town where everybody knows everybody. But she was one of our regulars, known to us all. She was a tall, exceptionally good looking, delightfully blonde lady whose home was in a small Alabama town up the road.

We never saw her well-to-do professional husband, but she loved to come to the beach. They owned a little place on the island when it was bare of all but a handful of tiny beach cottages. She also loved to drink and party. We'd see her in the popular spots around town...often tipsy ... always laughing ...always having a good time.

Needless-to-say, in a military town, an inebriated, good looking wife dancing around in bars is a magnet, a train wreck waiting to happen, figuring in the carousing, wild-assed, womanizing fighter pilot types plague-like among us then. We'd seen them leave far too many broken homes, broken hearts, and unplanned offspring behind.

We all watched her in sidelong glances... sure "that" had to be going on. There was an odd circumstance though. We never seemed to "catch" her in a liaison. She was always at her own table, alone. She was certainly happy, smiling, friendly, talkative... as well as tipsy, sometimes more than so. When someone asked, she might dance... but always, she went back to her table alone... and left the same way. Still, we were sure she had to be "slipping around" with one of our country's handsome, charming, witty, persuasive, wandering heroes. I mean... after all, weren't all the babes hanging around Eglin Air Force Base doing it?

Dawn seemed to have crept up on us faster than usual that Monday night...Tuesday morning, by then. When my boss and I headed for the door, there were just the three of us "patrons" left in the Indian Mound Saloon.

"Boy! She's worse than usual" my boss whispered.

"UhHuh. Awful wobbly." I replied glancing at her.

"Not safe for her to drive."

"I guess she usually gets home someway."

"We can't let her drive like that..."

"What...? We can't...?"

"Here. You take my keys." Reaching out to help others, on the spur of the moment, was so like him.

Words slurred, far more than unsteady on her feet, she didn't protest as he helped her to the passenger seat of her car.

"Aha!!!" I chortled as I followed, trailing along in his car. "Now... we'll find out what's... what!"

Not long married, I had no...zero... interest in being involved in the least of anything indiscreet. But, curiosity about this lady was rampant in town. Maybe we'd get, at least, a hint. And with my boss, my friend, I was certain we couldn't get into "trouble."

Bruce Ranew, my boss, the advertising and circulation manager for the Playground News, was one of the finest men I've ever known. His wife, Joyce, has always been one of the prettiest ladies in town. He loved her and his two small children dearly, his family always first, foremost in his concerns. Curiosity was decidedly not what motivated him that early morning. It was sincere concern for the safety of another.

We crossed the old Brooks Bridge and turned right onto what is now Santa Rosa Boulevard. On the near barren island, I eased to a stop beside her car in the sandy, seagrass swaddled yard, common to the few beach cottages out there then.

She was still mightily unsteady, wobbly, as she slouched out of the car seat and careened toward the door of the cottage. Her key scratched, scraped, clicked as she tried feebly to center it in the lock. At last... the door swung open. Hesitantly, we stepped inside, barely. Puzzling, odd... lights glowed brightly, all over the little house, flooding a kitchen-dining-living room area, and one bedroom. Without word...or pause, she stumbled through the living area to the bedroom and flopped onto the bed.

Eyes widening with obvious incredulity, my boss backed up a step toward the still open front door, jolting into me as he did so.

"Aaahaaa...!!!" It was an inordinately silent "Aha!" but loud, trumpeting, in my own astounded inner acumen. I mean..., wasn't this the "evidence" the boy's in town had whispered about?

As it happened, it turned out to be the briefest, the most evanescent, the most fleeting "Aha" in the "Aha!" dominion.

You see... at that very moment another bedroom door slammed open. With the explosive energy of a tornado another burst into the room with us. She was not as tall as the lady on the bed, but... far more than made up for it in beam. Eyes fiercely wide, piercing, angrily defiant, ebony face contorted in a temper that would have left a 300 pound defensive guard squirming in his shoulder pads, she rushed, barreled toward us. The words "train wreck" surged again to mind that night, rather alarmingly this time. Behind, in the room from which she'd just launched herself, I saw the beds of several sleeping children.

"Jes what is you genemans doing in dis house...???"

I gave my boss, my pal, all the help I could muster, backing hastily out the front door, giving him plenty of room to articulate the beneficence of our purpose.

Things quieted down pretty quickly. Bruce was always straight forward, quiet, proficient, soft spoken in dealing with everyone...always the good salesman. I stood outside in the gray light of morning, clutching the door knob.

Car keys made a soft metallic sound as he handed them over. Finally, I heard her thank him, a bit tentatively perhaps, for our courtesy, for bringing the lady of the house home safely. Obviously, it wasn't totally unexpected, not the first time she'd come home in similar condition.

We drove silently down the old island road, rolled across Brooks Bridge, back onto Main Street.

"Well..., there's sure nothing been goin' on in that house...!" I muttered.

"What the heck are you talking about ?" His face turned toward me, quizzical, truly puzzled. "So...? She has a little too much to drink sometimes!"

"Give her credit." I sighed. "She knows herself well enough to bring someone with her who'll keep her out of trouble."

Bruce Ranew was an excellent advertising and circulation manager. In our finite business world he was one of the best known on our Emerald Coast of those years, daily in and out of our little stores and offices, up and down Main Street, and Beal Street, and Eglin Parkway making his Playground News advertising rounds.

In like estate, his avocation was to be one of the best fried mullet cooks in town, in a time when that modest fish was often the mover and shaker of our social events. He was always ready to get out his big deep fat fryer and help with a fund raiser or social event.

When Bruce left the Playground News to start his own newspaper in Valparaiso, Wayne Bell promoted me to advertising manager. In youthful pomposity, I was sure I was good. Truly, though, I knew Bruce Ranew was better, more sure in sales talent, quietly persuasive in personality.

He left this life, and his loved family, much too young, the victim of a heart ailment that had also taken his father at an early age.

She and her family turned out to be simply among the first of a vastly growing flood of affluent folk who bought vacation homes along the beach because they love the Playground Area, the Miracle Strip, the Emerald Coast as much as we do. In fact, over the years, her name became something of an occasional, but regular, mention in Claude Jenkin's "Town Crier" society column.

The Indian Mound Saloon drifted along for years until Bill William's passing. Sometime after, the City of Fort Walton Beach bought it, ripped it asunder... it's place now filled by the entrance to our Indian Temple Mound and it's renowned museum.

All that's left, as far as this writer knows, is the big picture of the Indian Mound Saloon and old Main Street that fills a page of "A Miracle Strip," the photographic history of Fort Walton Beach produced by Tony Mennillo and his famous father's Arturo's Studios.

I often reminisce about the Indian Mound Saloon, and the ways of our far more Spartan Emerald Coast, a half century past now. How fortunate we are, it seems to me, when our youth is graced by friends like Bruce Ranew who enlighten through quiet example, teaching us to reach out in honor, and integrity, and caring, to all of those around us... no matter their circumstance.

ABOARD THE SLOOP *MORNINGSTAR*!

Of a clear, sunny, summer morning she'd slide free of her bonds, nudged along by the chattering of a tiny, smoky, British Seagull outboard. Our years together were a lifetime of those delightful castings off.

Just beyond the grasp of finger-like piers we'd steer into the south wind, down-haul halyards that lifted her mainsail to the sky. At the moment rippling canvas was taut against the mast top we, and Morningstar, belonged to the wind.

Hurry and effort slipped away in the headlong silence of engine shutdown, and she'd lie quietly, hove-to in the zephyr, waiting patiently for us to tilt the propellor clear and make everything else ship-shape for sea.

Then we'd turn her loose, let her bow drift 'round 'til the south wind was behind us, wing her mainsail far out to catch the force of the breeze. Straining muscles ballooned the cloud-white parachute of her Genoa jib two stories tall, and as the wind wafted us with gathering speed past the piers, Morningstar seemed to toss her bow with disdain at big shiny boats still clutched sleepily to weathered gray moorings.

Near silently we'd glide past the line of piers, the thick, steel, high-pointed arm of the boat lift, the short white-sand swimming beach, the round porch-like summerhouse. At the reedy tip of land we'd round Smack Point, haul the wind abeam. Daring each other, we'd skim boldly close to where the sand suddenly shelved into deep water, hard-racheting the cockpit winch that drew sky-high billows of canvas into a tight near-humming arc. Morningstar would surge ahead, heeling with dancer's grace as the weight of the wind shifted from stern to side. In those first moments of freedom there was silence save the growing whisper of wind on sail, the creak of taut rigging, the hollow, petulant lap-lap-lap of wavelets against the hull.

Yes..., in every life there should be one intense joy. A soul-mate may well be high on that roster of fulfillment, wife or husband who anchors existence and measures with us life's wonders. Home, family, faith, work that fine tunes skill and wisdom, might follow close behind. Still, there should be another passion, an aching dream, an unlearned understanding, a need as mysterious and compelling as the mistress, a desire that finds unexpected soul-depths, and lifts one's being out of humdrum of the everyday.

"There's one we'll never have..!," we said the first time we saw her. She was sleek and shapely and graceful enough. But, about her there seemed a frailness, an openness, a lack of guile, a faulting of the toughness a mistress should have. Those things, at first curious glance, made her unbecoming, un-beckoning. It was a brash unfairness, a hurried misjudgement that we'd remember with laughter many a time.

A part of her is to see that the rending of a family is an agony ...even when it becomes the only sensible destination. But, before the freed can soar, before healing and growing, before the charting of a new life-course, there must be tending of the young, of nestlings not yet ready to fly. In a way, it was the thing that brought her to us, shaped our years together, made her a glorious force in our lives.

The rounding out, the fullness, the majesty that made her whole is scarce measured as we know time. For eons our land was nurtured by so few, hidden away in an unsought corner of America, found by the many of us through fear and war. Her emerald green, in a sense, is a thing apart. Yet it rocked and cradled, let her slip quietly, sometimes roiling, through it's nurturing stream. It was Northwest Florida's sea-wind, sometimes swift moving, often gentle, blowing salt-tang to the taste, that bowed tall canvas to heeling submission, breathed into her the life we knew so well.

Lessons of Holy Trinity should have reminded that He was called The Morningstar. Somehow, we'd forgotten. We were glad, when it came to us, that His name was part of her. We made her our own with famed old verse: "give me a tall ship, and a star to steer her by."

She seemed majestic. In truth, she was just two inches over 23'. The other Morningstar, her mentor, was 100' of sleek sailing yacht, ocean racing from California to Hawaii in the early 1950's.

Some thought the Fort Walton Yacht Club pricey, a haughty place where human worth might be measured by the size of a bankroll.

We found it a sensible hideaway. On the peaceful mile-wide cove inside Smack Point she could lie quietly in wait for us, peering down thirty miles of open water.

Years before, it was the center of the town's high social life. But then, local folks had abandoned it to those far-early retired, some still clutching the surly arrogance of military command. As it happened, we were familiar with their habit and understood their talk of the air. And they'd come to love our sea. So we gathered just as sailors and bragged of our boats and drank green beer on St Patrick's Day.

It was a place that broadened the peace and freedom of a tiny apartment into wide-open windy spaces of bay and cove and shoreline. Far more, it was time and place to share with children when we were no longer together at every bedtime prayer.

We'd guessed, that first misguided glance, that Morningstar was lightly built, tippily unstable in the wind. The surprise, the truth of her made us laugh with embarrassment at our doubts. She was 3,000 pounds strong, 1,250 pounds of that, more than 40% of her, sleekly shaped deep keel that gave her the balance and power of a ballerina.

Northwest Florida's Winter winds, roiled over land and forest are turned shifty, treacherous, gusting unexpectedly. Morningstar might reel away from the chilly blast. But her deck, held upright by the weight of iron below her waterline, was never driven awash like those of larger, uppity, fine-yacht sisters.

Aye, in nimble, winning ways though, Morningstar was as fine-yacht as any of them, known and solemnly respected by all who could forthrightly call themselves sailors. Born in Canada of the famous house of O'Day, she came in '67 to the Emerald Coast's wind-swept Choctawhatchee Bay, to share so many years of her life and ours. In '75, we were third to call her our own, but we were family far longer than the others.

Before her there was a catamaran, a quick-sailing little watery steed meant to steer the young far from feared misdeeds of teenage years. It was a fast, exciting way to sail. In cooler seas and brisk Autumn winds, though, it's low canvas deck was a wet, teeth-chattering place. And so, the hope for one larger and drier took hold in our minds. In July she took hold of our hearts.

In the strange way of things it was just two months after she came that Eloise blew in on us, sucked the sea out of our bay, and sent it rushing back in a bruising eight foot wall of salty water. That hurricane lady, late in September, wrecked the docks and dumped most of the sailor's big beautiful toys in a crushed pile against a seawall. After the terrible rush of wind we found Morningstar, high and dry as a dead fish, lying on grass of the Yacht Club lawn. It cost near the price of her dowry to fix leaks and cracks, but so many others were lost, and she was still with us. That was all that mattered.

Morningstar never wandered far from her home, little more than the six or seven miles east that took us abaft the north shore of Destin.

Her cabin was called "cuddy" with bare sitting headroom, two bunks, head, and a glossy lacquered cabinet that might someday hold a galley. It was comfortable enough to wait out a rain shower, or to warm awhile from a cold wind, but such cramped quarters and lack of storage or winter heat made overnight cruising less than appealing. Freed of the mundane routines of living aboard we lived the intense joy of sailing, just for the sake of it.

Sailors hold the rushing power of nature in the puny grasp of human hand, humbly coerce wind and sea to send us where we want to go. Perhaps even more, to sit haunch-braced against wind-heeled craft, to grip guiding tiller and main sheet, is to fuse with 3,000 years of human wandering before the noisy engines we know. In the tall reach of white canvas we can see for ourselves how continents were found and peopled, how goods and gold were traded, how fortunes were amassed. We can feel thousands of journeys set forth, generation upon generation, when stars and sun were the sailor's only guide to make landfall and homecoming.

When the wind was easy, Choctawhatchee Bay flat and calm, we'd drape a suntanned leg over gray, furrowed wood of the tiller, lean back against cockpit coaming, let Morningstar ride with the breeze toward the long shallows of Lake Lorraine Point a mile or so to the east.

Now and then, a half dozen racing, cavorting gray shapes - near half the length of the sailboat - would appear beside us, touching close. They'd dart alongside Morningstar's bow, race ahead, criss-cross in front of us, arc with pleasured grace out of the Bay, bodies glistening with quick-flowing wet, grinning at our plodding pace. "Nawthuners" might call them Dolphin. To Northwest Floridians they've always been Porpoise. In the big pool of Fort Walton Beach's 'Gulfarium' the Porpoise will float erect, head above water, and gaze deep into human eyes with all the interest and care and understanding of an Irish Setter.

On a morning when the wind was hard from the sea, we could scarcely wait to sail round the wide shoals of Smack Point and head south again, into the rushing wind. Weathered posts, deep in sheltered brine, hold high the bright green face of Intra-Coastal Waterway marker #2. It's long, hard-working, two or three miles upwind made us pity first-time sailors on rented Hobie catamarans. We'd pass them unmoving, sails flapping flatly, uselessly, pointing vainly into the wind toward the rental dock. A sailboat can't sail directly into the wind.

Young sailors learn that going windward is a zig-zag course -"tacking" is the nautical word - sailing back and forth at an angle of 45 degrees or so until, finally, the landing is approached from aside. The distance is longer...but the excitement, the joy, is in getting there!

Sailing at 5 ½ knots, into 15 knots of breeze means 20 knots of wind in the teeth, sails winched down in taut vibrating arcs, sailboat heeled hard over, blustering through steep little walls of salty water marching in relentless oncoming rows. The fishy, salt tang scent of the ocean is impaled in sea spray, shouldered into the air by the splashing of the bow, blown back with the wind until faces are wet, sunglasses misty. A fast, sharp turn at each end of the zig-zag is heady exhilaration.

The boat rolls quickly upright, pitching sharply up and down in waves as the bow swings rapidly through the eye of the wind. Two-story tall canvas flaps and snaps like the crack of a whip, and the metallic clatter of the boom is menacing as it swishes past inches overhead...'til she staggers with the weight of new wind in her sails, heels deeply, eagerly onto the new course, gathers speed again.

The youngest of sailors learn to read the wind, not only in power and direction, but in it's water-ghost...the darker, moving, cloud-like shape, a rippled oval pattern on the calm sea surface that murmurs of a coming breeze.

The same water-ghost atop wind rushed waves shouts of a heavier gust on the way...precious time to ease the mainsheet, to head-up into the wind, to save the boat from heeling too far in the blow.

Knowing the sea itself is to sense the gathering effect of tide and wind and wave. On the Emerald Coast it's deeper secrets whisper through altering shades of green and blue to a sea floor of glistening white sand. In a few inches the water seems drinkable clear. In a foot or two it turns a glowing emerald, greening darker with depth, more vibrant in hue. In eight or ten feet, it gives way to the slate sea-blue that those from other shores know. For Morningstar's brood, it was easier to spot Northwest Florida's emerald green shoals, to spare her the humiliation of running aground.

"Red sky at morning, sailors take warning!" was the ancient mariner's wariness of the sea's danger. On the Emerald Coast, pale blue, bright sun, and cottony cloud above the mast top still bode well for a good day's sail, unless the chance violence of a summer thunder storm is smuggled in.

Hints of wind and sky and sea pilot a hope to master nature's power, to steer the vessel far away from trouble, past the turbulence of storm, into a fair wind and a calm, sheltered mooring. Is it any wonder that life's ebb and flow is likened to the sea...or that the young who sail are those who seek tomorrow's stars?

Her family days seemed lingering then, everlasting. But sunrise and sunset have a way of gathering, surprising. Far sooner than we know, they're stacked untidily one behind the other, a long queue of yesterdays, half-open drawers with remnants of memories poking out like old well-worn clothes.

Glancing astern we might see shadows of fear or joy, sadness, triumph, dear faces, things that have enriched, haunted, the time we're given.

There were two decades of them before we knew. By then, it was easy to see she far surpassed the task that was asked of her. They were youngsters, in the long ago when she came, fifteen and eleven and five. Curious it seems, since yesterday, they're grown to man and woman.

It is tanned and strong she reared them, stalwart and steady and self reliant they've grown. Each, like their father, has gone away and come home again...to the nature, the steamy loveliness, the seaside, the ocean wind, the backwoods country of Northwest Florida.

Morningstar taught them well, and they were wise to heed. In the passage of grown up lives, they know the value of teaming close and pulling hard together when the wind is up, to count the dangers and plot a course before safe mooring is cast aside. They know when lines are loosed and the pier slips far behind we must be ready...with all the knowledge and skill and passion and determination we've been given...to find our way safely, alone.

Too soon comes a time when the captain seems stodgy, the ways of childhood slow, old fashioned, when the excitement of the new looms high.

For awhile, one by one, they slipped away to good friends of youthful years, to more exciting pursuits...to fast Hobie Cats and noisy boats, part-time jobs, computers, cars...to education, and the shaping of new families. In the sprouting of generations, it must be that way.

They were missed, then, more than words can say. Yet, alone with the wind and the sea a sense endured, flourished, breathed a soul of it's own...Morningstar's favor to the captain himself. Long before she came to counsel the young, there had been the long-held, mute, unlikely dream. In every passion the finding, the knowing at last, the doing, the surmounting... might well become the intense joy, the fullness, the contentment every life hopes to know. The sail and the blue-emerald sea and the wind and the sandy reaches of Northwest Florida became, simply..., a joyful way of life.

Often through her years, near sundown..., tacking home into a gusty southwest wind fragrant with the scent of the sea, Morningstar heeled rail-down to rushing water, sails winched hard and tight and humming, the late evening breeze finally cooling the raging heat and humidity of Northwest Florida's summer...there would come the over-whelming sense of God's presence and gifts and peace.

AN EMERALD COAST DEED
TO REMEMBER!

Is it mere human vanity, a lofty perception of our importance to the world around us? Or maybe it's just the instinct of self preservation that gives us - for awhile at least - the mute smugness that our own dreams and aims and exploits are somehow momentous, everlasting.

But then...it's the slow, steady unfolding of years, the comings and goings of those around us, that unlimbers the knowing, acceptance, that our toils, our moments and thoughts and loves and annoyances will somewhere, sometime slip away...,at least from this world we know.

Still, there are those who accomplish things so pivotal, so vital, as to be truly unforgettable...or so it seems at the time.

In larger, long settled societies statues of granite or bronze tell their stories for a millennium or two. Here on the Emerald Coast mushrooming, overwhelming growth and the flowing, ever changing flood of new people have buried our short history. Deeds of early leaders live only in dusty bins of fading records that few ever see or know.

As years have piled up like a stack of old, yellowed newspapers, he has become a shining symbol of the loss. When we were so small, so unknown, so insignificant, he built something so big, so important, so visible to our hope of growth and prosperity that his name became a part of it, we thought, for all time.

Before the headlines, many of us already knew what he meant to do. Word of mouth has always been a powerful way of linking people and ideas, especially in a tiny town. For months he went door to door, store to store, talking up the impossible, pleading for support and donations, shaping the dream, slowly - bequest by bequest - making it our dream.

Lee Martin was one of the two best known saltwater sport fisherman in Fort Walton in those years. Not that there weren't a lot of fishermen then. Niceville and Destin were full of them, villages centered on fishing. But commercial fishing was their thing. In Niceville the boats brought in huge catches from the Gulf of Mexico to be shipped out to fish markets miles away. One or two sailing schooners, the old fishing smacks, could still be seen crossing Choctawhatchee Bay in those years, headed through Destin's East Pass to the Gulf. In Destin, commercial angling was for the pleasure of others, hauling vacationers who paid to go deep sea fishing.

Lee Martin and Bob McCreary fished because they loved it. With rod and reel they cast into the surf along the beach, looking for wily, delectable Pompano. Other times they'd be in small boats over grass beds in bay or bayou fishing for speckled trout and white trout and flounder.

Bob McCreary's Bay Store, downtown on Main Street, was as well known to the rest of us as our homes. "HARDWARE & FISHING TACKLE", the sign out front claimed, but there was far more tackle than hardware. In those easy going years we wouldn't have been surprised to find a note on the door saying, "gone fishing". Bob McCreary was hard working, an old Sears & Roebuck manager, but he wasn't above that when the Pompano were hitting. Usually, though he and Lee were out on the beaches when the sun came up, and back again in time for opening. Lee worked for George Alford at Leo's Men's Store, a few doors down Main Street. Fine quality tailored suits and shoes were his specialty. He and his wife lived in a house on Santa Rosa Sound at the west end of town where Main Street's Highway 98 became a highway again.

Early in 1952, radio was yet a few months away from Fort Walton, the Playground Area of Northwest Florida. Crestview had the only station. Television was an unstable flickering, beamed unpredictably from New Orleans without even a hint of local matters. Community tidings were spread by a weekly newspaper - one of Florida's finest by the way - the Playground News, tempered these 50 years into the powerful Northwest Florida Daily News we know today.

Then, it was only the headline, the news scoop, the reporter's words that brought an idea alive, made it real, important, the harbinger of things to come. The Playground News first mentioned it on February 14, 1952. It was Thursday, the day the weekly always came out. A small front

107

page article whispered that Sam Lindsay, president of the Chamber of Commerce had announced the formation of the Fort Walton Pier Association for the purpose of soliciting funds to build a fishing pier reaching out into the Gulf of Mexico. Sam, also a City Councilman and later Mayor of Fort Walton Beach, ran an insurance agency.

The news report mentioned Lee Martin as the man heading the campaign to raise money and announced that a permit had already been obtained.

It said another thing, a thing astonishing to those who did not share those years. The Town of Fort Walton pledged $2,500 toward construction, and agreed to maintain the pier. In fact, the Pier was to be built way out on the beach, a mile outside the boundaries of Fort Walton.   Truth is, Fort Walton-ites of those early years nurtured the whole area...Shalimar, Cinco Bayou, Mary Esther, Okaloosa Island, Destin...as their own. In fact, it was Fort Walton's Playground Area Chamber of Commerce that worked to build all of the Playground Area.

A week later on Thursday, February 21, 1952, banner headlines blazed across the front page of the Playground News, "WORK STARTS ON $27,000 FISHING PIER." Smaller headlines explained, "Municipal Pier To Extend Into Gulf 700 Feet." An even smaller subhead said, "45 Days Needed To Finish Work; Town To Manage."

This time the article named Lee Martin as the promoter and fiscal agent for the Fort Walton Pier Association. Theo Staff, head of the Staff's Restaurant family, was named as president. "Construction of the city's new $27,000 municipal fishing pier started this week...," the reporter wrote, "...at the Newman Brackin Wayside Park, site of the pier."

Donations both large and small, the Playground News revealed, could be made by contacting Lee Martin at telephone number 2-3611 or Box 57, Fort Walton.

The Pier was to be 12' wide, 700' long, with 600' extending out into the Gulf from the water's edge. Keenan Co., engineers for the City of Fort Walton, were in charge of construction.

For the next five weeks the Playground News was silent about the Fort Walton Municipal Pier. Lee Martin, though, stayed very busy making personal visits to area merchants. Shalimar Center, a neighborhood trio of drug/ sundry, package liquor, and automatic laundry stores, was owned by my parents E.A. and Iris Baughman. I, the "soda jerk", ran the drug store's lunch counter and soda fountain. Shalimar is two miles from Fort Walton, but Lee Martin came in often on his rounds and my parents donated to the pier fund. Lee always bought a double dip vanilla ice cream cone. Most men smoked in those years but Lee had a curious habit. He smoked and ate at the same time, exhaling cigarette smoke directly onto the ice cream. Non-smokers would wince to see him do it.

Support for the pier grew rapidly. The appeal of Lee Martin's idea was obvious, resounding. Local fishermen and vacationers could fish 600' out in Gulf waters, standing firm and dry on the deck. Surf fisherman could cast out less than 100', wet and often cold, waist deep in rolling waves.

"Already, we have classified 16 species of edible fish that are in the waters around the pier," Lee Martin said, "and I believe there are more." The pier would bring more vacationers to spend money on motels, restaurants, fishing tackle, souvenirs.

But the Playground News issue of April 17, 1952 brought bad news. "Worked has stopped on the pier," Lee Martin was quoted as saying, "because there is no money to pay the men."

Two weeks later, the issue of May 1, 1952 brought news that was, for awhile at least, a bit better. "Enough money has been raised," Lee Martin said, "for two more weeks work." In addition, the Playground News reported that the Fort Walton Women's Club had scheduled a "free will offering dance" at the Shalimar Club on Friday night May 2nd. Donations were for pier construction.

Two things about that event were far from surprising. First, the Fort Walton Women's Club levied a powerful voice, a strong social conscience, in the early development of the Playground Area. Second, Roger and Ella Clary, who owned the Shalimar Club, were at the top of the list of early leaders who guided us to where we are today. Their business and social contributions to our area development were, and continue to be, immense. The Shalimar Club, in the tiny village of Shalimar, was one of the most elegant night clubs in the South, with red-coated waiters in formal attire. Andy Griffith, now long-famous as a star of TV and films, appeared there. "What It Was, Was Football", and "Swan Lake" and several other hilarious monologues brought him national fame in the early '50's. We saw Andy Griffith perform them on the Shalimar Club's gleaming wood dance floor.

Three more weeks of Playground News silence slipped by. Pier construction forged ahead and Lee Martin continued his rounds of fund raising. He'd been joined by his fishing buddy Knute McCulley who owned the Pure Oil station three doors down Main Street from Leo's Men's Store.

Knute had drifted down from Atlanta, fallen in love with the fishing and nature and quiet of Fort Walton, and bought the auto service business. He, too, made calls seeking building funds and his Pure Oil station became a second headquarters for the effort. "A lot of people," Knute recalled recently, "dropped donations off there."

The Playground News issue of May 22, 1952 showed clearly how widespread community support for Lee Martin's idea had become. Mr. And Mrs. H.J. Benkirt of LaRue Frock Shop on Main Street, wrote the Playground News reporter, contributed 10% of their last Friday's sales to the Pier construction fund. "The Pier is for all of us," Mrs. Benkirt said, "we hope other merchants will do the same." Lee Martin was quoted, too. "Good progress was made on construction this week," he said, "and the Shalimar Club dance brought us between $200 and $300."

A big, two column, photo of Lee Martin, Theo Staff, and J.V. Calvin dominated the front page of the June 12, 1952 issue. Calvin was treasurer of the Pier Association. Lee a slender, rangy man, stood a head taller than the others. The black and white photo doesn't show it, of course, but Lee was always darkly tanned from long hours of fishing in the Northwest Florida sun. His voice was deep-toned, strong. The aura about him was one of self assurance and authority. His casual dress was often a nautical sport shirt, white pants and yachtsman's cap.

"LEE MARTIN PIER," a headline under the photo proclaimed. On that day, the Playground News reporter wrote:

"Fort Walton Pier Association members, Monday, officially designated that as the official name for the municipal fishing pier on Santa Rosa Island."

"Mr. Martin has done more than anyone else to promote the pier for the area," Theo Staff was quoted as saying, "the Pier is the biggest thing here in several years." The Fort Walton Motor Speedway, the old racetrack for which Racetrack Road is named, scheduled wrestling matches for June 24th with a percentage of the gate going to the Pier fund. It was also noted that the Magnolia Club on Main Street gave 20% of it's Tuesday night's proceeds. The Magnolia, located at the corner of Main Street and Perry Avenue where the Publix mall stands today, was the other classy nightclub in the Playground area.

"We've already completed 600'...," Lee Martin said, "...and we're going to add another 150', making it 850' in all. The pier should be open to the public on July 4th, if weather permits."

Yet again, on July 10, 1952 the Playground News brought bad news. "$900 more is needed," Lee Martin announced. "The Pier won't be opened until enough money is donated to back the payroll for two more weeks. "Last week," he said, "I had to shell out of my own pocket to finish meeting the payroll, and I don't plan to do that again. A dime, quarter, dollar, or five - whatever anyone wants to give - will be appreciated."   Presently, the Playground News reporter continued, workmen are constructing a 70-foot "T" at the end of the 710-foot Pier. It was clear the extra 150' had been quickly abandoned because of a shortage of money.

"DEDICATION SET FOR MARTIN PIER," blared a two column Playground News front page headline on Thursday, July 17, 1952.

And the following week's issue confirmed it. The "LEE MARTIN PIER" was opened to the public on Friday, July 18,1952 at 10:00 a.m. The news photo was too big to overlook. It pictured Lee Martin and his wife standing on the long deck, his yachtsman's cap set jauntily on his head. He held scissors, ready to cut the red ribbon that opened the Pier to the public. Mrs. Martin's high heels seemed a bit out of place on the roughness of the boards, but her smile was

gracious. Of all their sunrises and sunsets before and after...,
that day belonged to them. The skirt of her pretty off-the-
shoulder sun dress rippled in the sea wind...a lovely breeze,
unchanged these 50 years.

She held a bottle of champagne at the ready,
determined to smash it over the railing as though launching
a 700' ship.

Pastor Johnson Pace of downtown St. Simon's-on-
the-Sound Church gave an invocation, and Fort Walton Mayor
O.M. "Pete" Earley made the dedication speech.

"It is a dream come true," Mayor Earley said, "fulfilled
by many people. But, it was Lee Martin's hard work that
made the dream come true." Theo Staff, president of the
Fort Walton Pier Association was quoted one final time. "Lee
Martin deserves all the credit," he declared, "he got the thing
started and pushed it by himself. It is only fitting that it bear
his name."

Mrs. Martin, said the Playground News reporter, gave
the champagne bottle a healthy whack on a corner of the
Pier. On the second try, the bottle split a concrete block.
Then, on the third, the bottle bounced off a post. On the
fourth she grabbed the neck of the bottle tightly and shattered
it.

"You can see," Lee Martin commented wryly, "this Pier
is going to be here a long time."

And so it was. For twenty five or thirty years, more
than a quarter of a century, to those of us who knew the
truth, it was the "Lee Martin Pier." Hundreds of us, and
thousands of visitors, walked it's plank deck, delighted in it's
ocean scent, caught it's fish, gripped it's rails unsteadily in
gusty wind and rain to see the big waves of a coming
hurricane. Lee Martin's Pier more than surpassed the dream
itself.

And then, a decade or so ago, the Pier passed to
Okaloosa County Commissioners...in Biblical terms, to those,
"who knew him not."

Millions were spent on the fancy concrete pier, built
anew on the other end of Wayside Park. In their unknowing,
in haste, Commissioners had forgotten all he had
achieved...all we had done.

Suddenly, there was a new name, a trendy corporate name...the Okaloosa Island Pier. It is, it seems to this troubadour of our brief history, a bland name, a cold name, a name without flesh and blood, without the toil or hope or worry or doubt that shaped it's sire.

It is a name that spews our past out of it's mouth, and violates the tales of what we were, of how we came to be.

There were just 2,388 in Fort Walton in 1950, certainly a few more in 1952 when Lee Martin built our Pier. So many, our elders, have danced their dance upon life's stage and left us to finish our journey alone. There are few, now, to complain.

Still when the wind is up and the song of the surf rouses the sea air along the beach we might heed their voices if we listen closely. Those of us who shared those years know what we'd hear.

"Give us, at least, our remembrance," they'd murmur. It would be a kind, tempered, unaffected murmur... for that's the way most of them were. You see, our imperious, affluent, latter day emigres have inherited magnificence that was far from easily earned. In hubris they breeze over the verity... that in those early years it was crafted with so little money..., far more with toil and hope and dreams.

Lee Martin's name, today, should stand tall on the Pier. His titan accomplishment was a symbol for all of us, for each and every one of the modest, daily, forgotten labors that forged our lives together in the 1950's and built this delightful land we've called the Playground Area, the Miracle Strip..., the Emerald Coast.

A NIGHT IN THE CAGE

At the west end of Destin's bridge, outside the tiny saloon, he slid into the seat. Quick, sure movements of his hands and feet coaxed the machine to life. A going away party can be festive and sad, a coalescence of emotion. This one had turned out well, but he was glad it was done.

Red was not the dazzling of a fire engine, but rich burgundy that made the car gleam from his own prideful buffing. The white canvas top loomed ghostly pale in muted glows of past-midnight stars and a waning quarter moon. One lone, green-shaded, light bulb dangled on it's own electric cord above the doorstep of the little bar. Yet, it's faint-hearted, brooding, gleam added little to the velvet of night.

Dual mufflers lent a sweet, throaty purr to the gutsy V-8 engine. It was "souped up," as they put it in the mid-1950's, with Mallory coil and dual point ignition. Mud flaps, fake fender exhaust ports shiny with chrome, and a big spotlight mounted at the driver's window, added to the '49 Ford convertible's racy look.

The diminutive barroom, stood a good ways seaward from the road, girded by sand dunes and tall, slender sea oats nodding in deference to the ocean wind. Coarse sea-side grass grew raggedly onto crushed oyster shell, the miserly paving of the meager parking lot. It was a construction that was commonplace then.

Tires crackled, crunched, on the coarse shell, twin spiraling trails of lime dust following his tires as he eased up the shallow grade. The Ford bumped, lurched as it mounted onto inky asphalt of the road.

In seconds his speed was soaring, twin mufflers humming a deep bass timbre, as he bolted westward on U.S. 98 toward Fort Walton Beach six miles away. In late nighttimes of that pristine era, a car was a rarity between Destin and Fort Walton Beach. Highway 98 was formidably dark, a bare lonely stretch. Sand the color of sugar drifted out in hazardous windblown piles. White fiddler crabs often

114

scuttled in headlight beams on the raven roadway.

To coax the quick, agile, car to race always set his pulses pounding! Fifty...sixty...seventy miles an hour! It seemed to him that the big engine sang, the canvas of the convertible top vibrating audibly in the airstream above his head, the blacktop beneath him a fast running stream!

Eighty miles an hour!...he and the racing machine were one...hands, eyes, feet wedded to it's flying steel. It was as though it was he, not tires, that touched that streaking highway, sensing it's surface under him, feeling for its dangers, making minute corrections in their inseparable course.

Ninety miles an hour!... The wind around him was a rush of sound, the canvas top buzzing in fast streaming air inches above his hair. Highway 98 savaged into a black raging river, it's white dashes of center line near a twinkle as they blazed past headlight beams.

From where, came this wanton savor of speed? In the most frugal of personas it was his one imprudence... well, that, and the occasional swigging of a bit too much of the frothy brew.

Surely, love of moving fast came not from father or grandfather. He knew them and their joys well. Somewhere, he wondered, in his genetic inheritance could there have been a great-grandfather whose pulses raced at the feel of a fast powerful steed... an ancestor from a far different time who loved the feel of the wind in his face, the feel of muscles driven to their limit rippling beneath the saddle as he and that steed galloped as one, hooves drumming on an earthen lane?

Is that what we ponder as Dejavu? Will scientists, in future time, find a minuscule atom in some submicroscopic corner of our biological genes that carries memory from a far distant ancestor to us... memory that bequeaths unearned talent, deep unexplainable desire, perhaps one that might make sweet and dear and familiar a face we've never before seen?

One hundred miles an hour!...it was steely excitement to let it run, to hear the wind over the canvas, the whine of the engine, the hiss of the hot tires on asphalt, to feel the lift and roll of the car over the road's treacherous unevenness.

He held it at that flying peak for just a few exhilarating seconds, then throttled the big engine down, reveling in the low-pitched rumble of the dual mufflers as power tapered off.

The flutter of the canvas quieted. Wild wind rush became a whisper again as he rounded the last broad curve..., easing, slowing, drifting to a stop at the bridge over Santa Rosa Sound.

Black and yellow stripes, the span's lowered, wood-slat, safety barrier forbid his fervor, a warning bell jangling harshly. The roadway gaped awide, abandoned for the moment, leaving a broad dark watery gap where the center of the span had been. The old John T. Brooks bridge turned slowly, ponderously on a broad round center pedestal, taking it's share of the roadway for a ride until it was perpendicular to the rest of the highway. Only then could the creeping tugboats with long tows of barges grumble their way through.

He switched off the engine. The old swing bridge exacted patience, extorting moments of leisure, a thing lived daily by those who had to go to Destin or the beach in those years. Indeed, one might as well relax, sit through a few ordered holiday moments while the span was open. There was no other way.

Truth was, a lot of us groused about the delay, yet secretly relished the diversion. For a long gathering of pleasured minutes, he watched the white darting finger of the tug boat's searchlight pointing into the night, first here, then there, blazing a halo of intense light around each successive bobbing buoy that would guide it safely through the narrow channel. He never tired of watching tugboats go through...out into the bay... on to somewhere else. It was elementary to give a thought to being on board, to dream of going away with the unseen crew.

When, at long last, the tug and its barges had slipped past the open span of steel girders the old bridge rumbled its laborious way closed again. He and his fancy machine glided across the healed roadway, into the cozy, abridged, downtown of Fort Walton Beach.

At one o'clock in the morning in the 1950's, Main

116

Street had an air of mystery, a seductive half-awake ambience. Rustling palm trees lined each side of it's sidewalks. Barroom windows sported brightly hued, flickering neon signs. Winds that wandered in from the sea brought succulent ocean fragrance inland. Anywhere in town in those quiet years, when the surf was up, the crash and roar of breaking waves echoed over Santa Rosa Island, across the moon-traced narrows of Santa Rosa Sound, through deserted streets, to homes of those who knew little of air-conditioning... into open windows of the bedfast who'd been lulled to sleep by rhythms of the shore.

He glided past Ham's all night drive in restaurant, the Magnolia Club, Bishop's Bar & Lounge, The Flamingo Bar & Lounge. All - except Ham's, of course - were still an hour or so away from closing.

He glanced into darkened, dozing, enterprises... Echol's Furniture, Fortune's Hardware, Bob McCrary's Bay Store, Paul Robert's Rexall Drugs, Mary Cox's boarding house, Pete Earley's Ice & Seafood.

Between the booming Spanish Villa night club and where Frenchie's Restaurant used to be, he veered right, onto the sweeping curve to that led him north down Eglin Parkway, Highway 85, toward home.

Out Eglin Parkway stores were fewer, farther apart, darker, the street itself barely lit. On his left at First Street was the old Fort Walton schoolhouse. On his right, the Piggly Wiggly, Ratcliff's Firestone, and, next door, Mrs. Ratcliff's fine restaurant.

At the end of town as he passed the boulevard named for the more famous Hollywood, the street transfigured into rural road again, blending immediately into pine forest.

Spontaneously, almost of it's own volition, speed inched upward. Two miles later, barreling along over the bridge and bayou called Cinco, he and his machine were sprinting at 70... an ill-starred pace... 25 mph over the speed limit.

It wasn't that he failed to note the police car on the corner at the foot of Cinco bridge. "What the heck!" he muttered, "They've seen me already..." As time curdled, it turned out to be far from the best of decisions. "...might as well let 'er roll!" Thankfully, youth fuels such rash folly only a brief span of time, if our sensibilities grow apace.

"Anyway," he reassured himself, "I'll be over the Shalimar Bridge and out of their jurisdiction before they can get up to speed!" He slowed not the slightest! Far behind his tail lights, in the rectangle of his rearview mirror, he saw the blue chase lights begin to spin.

To his surprise he found himself chuckling aloud at the excitement of the hunt. Pulses pounding again, racing for the last bridge he flashed past Mom and Pop's Café in Ocean City where, on so many nights, he drank himself into peacefulness...past Luther Clary's Ocean City Cocktail Lounge, a blur of bright neon in a sea of pine trees...past the dim lights of scattered houses half hidden by thin forest.

He came upon it fleetly, abruptly, menacingly close, creeping slowly. Was it possible the city cops had radioed ahead to the dark blue Air Force police van? Suppose it veered, tried to block him at such speed? Might be the worst crash imaginable. Bravado was one thing! The flash of a second weighed odds not at all to his liking. Within sight of the Shalimar Bridge, he gave up the race, sliding the sleek machine to a halt in a cloud of dust on the roadside.

He fully expected a speeding ticket by then. Yet deluded by youthful candor, he'd vastly misjudged official anger and resentment caused by his eager willingness to race.

"Follow us back to the station," one of the two police officers snarled. Those were trusting years. Meekly, obediently, he and his humbled speedster trailed them the four miles back to the tiny town.

In September of 1954, Fort Walton Beach's City Hall was a meager, low, flat roofed white building on First Street, not far from the First Baptist, First Methodist, and St. Mary's Catholic Churches. As these words are penned in the year 2003, the old building serves as the City's art museum. City Hall long ago moved on to bigger, grander digs on Highway 98, Miracle Strip Parkway.

He sat, fidgeting in a hard, honey-oak, chair while lines of official paperwork were laboriously filled in, ignored except when asked gruff, pertinent, questions. It seemed unending. Finally it was done.

"You can make one phone call..." officers told him, still gruff, terse, impersonal.

Knowing well his father's despotic ways, it seemed far from a good idea to call him at 1:00 am to be gotten out of jail.

Better... perhaps far better, it seemed..., to let them worry a bit... wonder if he was injured or dead before discovering such an incredible blunder.

"Well..., I got myself into it..." he told the officers in tones more calculated than the swagger he feigned, "...I'll get myself out of it."

"Oookaaaay!!!" Blue-uniformed officers glanced knowingly at each other. Noticeable sarcasm in the voice of the one who answered should have been a warning to anyone even a bit familiar with "the law." He, of course, was not.

They guided him out a side door, across a narrow alley, to a small concrete block building behind, separate from the main City Hall building.

The first glimpse of prison can be nothing less than a jolt to any normally righteous being's sensibilities. He found himself looking down a short, narrow, hall with a queue of rusty iron bars on it's right side. Three cells. He counted them in a glance. Just one dim light, abjectly failing in it's contention with night, adorned the concrete block wall across from the row of cages. In fact, the light was so desolately poor it was impossible, at first, to see anything inside except the runty hall itself.

A massive key clinked in it's slot. Oversized hinges screeched caustically bearing a clatter of brawny metal. The harsh clang of stout bars behind, finding himself inside, seemed unreal, odd, dream-like.

Without a parting word the officers ambled out leaving him deserted, untended. In mere moments he would be far more than glad they had favored him with the cell nearest the door.

In 1950 the Fort Walton Beach census recorded just 2388 souls in residence. Municipal budgets, edged near non-existence, reflected a police department with three or so underpaid "officers", an elderly chief retired from the

Birmingham police force, and the barest minimum of "facilities." There was virtually no state or federal over-sight of local police ventures to assure detention comforts.

Solitude itself, though, was not strange, nor even disquieting to him. Dark had never seemed a nemesis. His growing years had been in the countryside, on a modest farm. Night, sans artificial glow, brightened only by nature herself, was fiercely familiar.

As his eyes grew accustomed to the constricting dimness, moonlight waxed to commanding prominence, it's welcome silver glow angled inward through the open door, an arms reach through the bars. Stars, twinkling in moon-brightened sky, wee gleaming recollections of Bethlehem, lightened a meager, barred window high on the concrete wall. Such gifts of the shadowed hours were old friends. He felt easy with them as he had on so many evenings of his life.

But then, he became aware of "it," enveloping him, permeating his very consciousness. "It" was abiding, alive, awesome, horrible, dreadful..., unbelievable! Were there civilized terms which might describe it...? Perhaps, say, an odor...,a smell..., a disagreeable redolence ?

This revolting reek...this foulness...this stink was far...far... from civilized! More than simple regression, it was utter rankness, a nauseating hint of times, eons ago, when men lived like..., and closely with..., beasts.

On the farm, he had slopped hogs in their wallows, cleaned and wheel barrowed away thousands of pounds of fresh, wet, chicken droppings, stumbled across roguish skunks in farm fields.

Unpalatable barnyard fragrances paled into timid, mousy insignificance in the rancid air, the rotting, fetid, cankering stench which assailed, ravaged his nostrils.

To be sure, as moments crept, he was certain he could feel the worst of disease-carrying viruses, bacteria, germs festering in his breathing passages. At first, in Fort Walton Beach's barbaric lair of those years, he felt sure he would choke to death!

Gagging, trying frantically to breathe as little as humanly possible, he pressed his face against cool bars as close to the open door as his nose could stretch.

There, with an occasional puff of clear, warm summer breeze, he could gasp a breath, a tinge of barely pure air... halfway, at best, undefiled.

Finding that modest source of un-fetid air awarded the barest, the runtiest, sense of soothing. Reborn with it, was a suggestion, barely a hint, of survival. Amid gasps of purer air, he began, like a blind man stumbling, to survey that insufferable place.

The pace of it was agonizing frustration. Ever so slowly his eyes acclimated to the near total lack of light, especially in the back of the cell. At last, barely, in side-wise glances he could make it out. Stunned with outraged disbelief he came to grasp the meaning of that horrid, unimaginable, overwhelming fetor.

You see, in Fort Walton Beach's jail of the 1950's there was no toilet. The wrenching, ungodly air emanated ..., radiated would be the better sense of it..., from a massive, marshy gathering of the very worst of human waste. Clearly now, it was human feces, urine, vomit, putrefying in a glossy mound in the left back corner of the cell floor.

Staring into the dimness at such an astonishing, unimaginable, disgusting discovery...wishing not to believe his eyes..., he was gripped by one minute sense of grate-fulness. At the very least, the drunks had the presence of mind to keep it all in one corner..., in one festering hoard.

Hardly worse, but just as surely, in Fort Walton Beach's jail, there was no wash basin, no source of drinking water, no chair, not even a custodian to aid the prisoner in the most basic of human needs. Sudden, critical, illness could easily bring death. No one cared.

Obviously, Fort Walton Beach in the 1950's felt that drunks, prisoners, had little human worth, or perhaps, would be in no condition to be aware of a need for sanitary "amenities."

In youthfulness, more naive perhaps than most, in his worst nightmare he'd never dreamed that humans, at least in our "government-of-the-people" America, could treat each other in such a way, even in rash impropriety.

There was a bed of sorts, the only place a hapless "occupant" might sit. But...no sheet, no cover, not even a pillow. Eyes straining in the dimness of the single distant light, he could see fearsome brown splotches on striped ticking of the metal cot's lumpy mattress. By then their cause was hardly in question.

He stood as long as he could, as long as his legs would hold him, repulsed at even the thought of touching those virulent looking stains.

Sudden rage swept over him at the animal-like environment, the choking stench he was caught within. It was a thing wildly unlike him, but he violently rattled the iron bars, hoisted himself to their top, craftily inspecting every weld, every hinge in the dim light, fleetingly hopeful he'd find a way out. He stood on the stained mattress and gave the tiny barred window the same intense attention.

Finally, conceding, accepting, he stood quietly, hands on the cool iron of the bars. It was a filthy, stinking, dehumanizing place. To the credit of it's makers, though, it was more than solid! For the briefest of moments, he was shaken by the fierce, bewildering sense of being trapped, helpless, powerless.

But then, just as quickly, frenzy ebbed, waned. In it's place grew an odd sense of serenity, of self control, of personal sufficiency, of doing what had to be done, firmly, quietly. It was a hardiness learned in his family far more by example than by mere words.

Was it an hour he'd been there? Two? Three?... when a fellow traveler in his finite universe of iron bars was half dragged through the open door, arms draped around the necks of the two cops, legs dragging with sorely drunken ungainliness. With that same rattling, clanging, the newcomer was locked in the third cell.

He quickly found his new friend to be the drunkest drunk, the roaring-est drunk, the happiest drunk he'd ever seen! In the small military town of Fort Walton Beach and it's busy saloons he had seen a world of drunks.

The starched glistening white uniform with its gold splashed shoulder boards, so different from the sky-blue threads of local ranks, made it clear that the new cell mate was from the Annapolis of the Air forty miles away.

They struck up an immediate camaraderie, the

122

fledgling Navy pilot and he. They were of like age and, at the moment, sharing the same dismal encounter. Of such things are friendships made.

For a time, perhaps an hour or so, they shared bits of their lives and experiences, yelling questions and answers across the gap of the empty cell. The young pilot was so reelingly drunk, so thick tongued, that they never introduced themselves beyond first names. It was never clear where his arrest occurred or why the "Navy" was partying so far from home base, except the not surprising hint that a local girl had been the object of pursuit.

One thing was clear. The young pilot was far too drunk to miss the nonexistent sanitary facilities or, luckily, to be aware of the horrible choking stink in the place.

They criticized cops in keenly unflattering terms, made light of their situation as best they could, laughed together as friends do, sometimes roaring with laughter at an especially funny comparison. Friendship may be for a lifetime, or effervescent, brief as a candle in spring breeze. Fashioned, engaging, it is always an overt sharing, lifting us up, boosting us on...a thing inescapably necessary for survival.

Together, for a while, they lightened the burden of those hours. After a time, when they'd shared all that had occurred to them... the young pilot began to sing.

Considering how knee-walking drunk the Navy was their blended voices seemed surprisingly good. Harmony echoed back and forth across the empty cell, between the bars, lending just the barest hint of culture to the barrenness of those cages.

Culture, that is, until the pilot began singing the most famous of all flying songs, one known to pilots in every branch of military aviation. In the way of culture it leaves a great deal to be desired, but it is a lusty tune made to be sung with great gusto. And...sing it with gusto they did, yelling out the chorus at the top of their lungs into the still warm early morning air.

"Roll me over, roll me over, roll me over lay me down and do it again!"

Over and over and over. No one came to arrest their loud, boisterous song. Likely police were accustomed to noisy drunks in the cage. Or maybe they were gone again...out on patrol, leaving City Hall fully unattended.

The young pilot's voice began to fade, grow more slurred, hushed. Soon, the sound of snoring replaced songs that had spanned the empty cell.

He wondered long after who the young pilot had been, whether he survived his flying. His happy outgoing personality, athletic good looks, most of all his chance to fly were things easy to esteem. In a way the pilot was like his boyhood friend who'd died the year before at twenty-one in a bomber crash in Newfoundland. He, like his boyhood pal and that Navy pilot, had ached to fly.

Fatigue, finally, took it's toll, ran it's course. Brown splotches on the lumpy mattress began to seem, somehow, less venomous. He sat down, hesitantly, uneasily on that unclothed, mangy cot... settled down to wait out the night, to see what might happen. It never occurred to him to call out for aid, to change the decision he'd made, to regret the speed, the chase, the savouir-faire!

Twenty-two hours awake, overpowered by the need for sleep, he finally gave in, lay down, surrendered to the ugly stains. Just as he drowsed into sleep there came softening of the dark, the first pale rose of dawn.

Scarcely an hour later, his mother and sister were there reaching through the bars, tugging his hair. They were laughing. Not of ridicule. He knew at once their laughter was of relief... that he was there, safe, even in that awful place, not injured or dead. In their close family, it was far more than an odd sight, one of them behind iron bars. They did not bail him out, though. In those years, that was still the job of the man of the house.

His father let him bide his time, ponder behind the bars, for several hours more...until Northwest Florida's mid-morning heat of a splendid, clear, September day.

To the young man's utter astonishment the usually wrathful sire spoke no criticism of his late-night inanity. Smouldering anger was directed, instead, at those who managed such an abominable place, caging his briefly wayward son without the least of food or drink. In fact he was angered enough to go to the expense of hiring an attorney for a simple appearance in traffic court.

Short tales of creative fiction might well have a sudden twist, an astounding discovery, a melodramatic surprise... for the end of it.

History, though, is just what it was... what that night was... what the old Fort Walton Beach jail was ...a graphic image of what the City could sometimes be a half century ago.

As a fact of history, though, the attorney turned out to be a very young man named Erwin Fleet, whose father, Nathan Fleet, for a very long time was proprietor of Fleet's Shoe Store on Fort Walton Beach's Main Street. "See Fleet to Fit Your Feet." Nathan was one of the best known of early Emerald Coast civic and business leaders, highly active, greatly respected.

Erwin Fleet became locally famous, widely admired and venerated, as one of our longest term Okaloosa County Judges.

Judge Joseph "Andy" Anderson, equally regarded as an early Emerald Coast attorney, and the first Judge of Fort Walton Beach's Municipal Court ruled in the case. The $60 in traffic fine and court costs drained the young offender's savings account, and justifiably so. It took a while, in those years, to accumulate that much.

Come to think of it, perhaps there may be an odd, ironic twist to what seems the most dismal of tales. Twenty years later our then youthful, one-night, jailbird became one of the highest elected officials in Fort Walton Beach.

By then, the mid 1970's, the City boasted one of the most modern, most immaculate, best managed small-city jail facilities in America.

In more than ten years as a Fort Walton Beach City Councilman and Mayor Pro Tempore, the City jail was a necessary governmental malevolence he could assess and support with pride, with much more than a little understanding. In fact, few could know more personally of the dark side of it.

In time, he sensed an infinite perception in the intensity of the dark hours. In the core of his being he found himself different, stronger... strength which grows imperceptibly, forging us into the winnow of flourishing humanity God wills us to be. Perhaps that night was his personal equinox, time when he was destined to become more man than boy.

For most, the cages in which we find ourselves are not of iron, but of the mind and heart, barring full measure of happiness, strangling great opportunities of our lives. And just as often the bars through which we peer are forged of our own fear... to be just ourselves, to be different, to stand alone, to try, to fail, to risk, to love. Life is a strange blend of those things..., gaiety and heartache, beauty, ugliness, excitement, patience, friendship.

The incongruity of that "night in the cage" was that he had somehow managed to experience it so much of it between one setting and rising of the sun.

By The Sea
in Shades of Night

Certainly, since America's Civil War..., perhaps since the first army took the field in the dim far reaches of human history, military camps have been wild, unfettered, free-spirited places.

It was in 1862 that General Joseph J. Hooker commanded the expansive Union Army garrison at Washington. "Camp-followers" was the name given them then...the willing, intimately generous girls who hung around army posts of those years. Circling close to General Hooker's bastion, they were so countless, so visible, Washingtonians linked their busy presence with the General himself. Ever since, "hooker" has been the slangy American word for ladies of the evening, the world's oldest profession.

Of course, in those more circumspect times, the linkage was likely a great disservice to one of our most distinguished Civil War Generals. In the swaggering, womanizing career military grown from the desperation and huge armies of World War II, it would be a fitting epitaph for many a military officer.

Not that there aren't a great many fine, dedicated, family-centered men and women under arms. Indeed there are, and each is worthy of the word "hero!" Military chaplains find their chapels filled with them on Sabbath days. The defense of our country hinges on their good sense and faithfulness and high moral values.

Yet, in the Emerald Coast's formative years, those who gave the troops a bad name were manifold, glaringly conspicuous. Bellied up to the bar in the happy hours of military clubs and downtown saloons, they shrouded the character of their profession with arrogance, brawling, womanizing, infidelity, drunken parties, gambling, neglected children, broken families. To those raucous souls peace meant time to waste, play came before work, and drifting here and there was a handsomely rewarded finesse.

In such an ambience of high living it wasn't surprising

to find damsels whose virtues might swoon like a palmetto in a hurricane before swaggering machismo, rank-haughty social status dazzling from uniform collar or sleeve.

In the late 1940's and 50's the tiny, two-fisted, hard-drinkin' military town of Fort Walton Beach was waist-deep in the caterwauling flamboyance of such irrepressible, liberated spirits. The proclivities of 10,000 freewheeling fly-guys often outweighed the modesty of little more than 3,000 Emerald Coast "live heres". And, of course, a beach town attracts a similar fast-moving multitude from among civilian "tourists."

Fort Walton Beach was, even then, a delightful place to live with lots of churches and a great many fine, honorable, hard working people.

At the same time, we've always had more than our share of hell-raisers.

So you see, even in those small town years it was considerably less than surprising to hear of a "lady" who might - how shall we say? - have a snort or two, too many, and become unclothed in the company of a man she'd met just hours before.

Into this slippery slope of ethical mobility, one day in the mid-1950's, rode a fellow whose business it was to sell advertising for the Florida Sheriff's Magazine. That was certainly a noble sounding livelihood, and he probably sold a good many ads on the day he blew into our seaside town. But whispers that flittered up and down Main Street the day after his resounding fiasco wondered far more about his notion of after-work entertainment.

Now, there's nothing of record to say whether he was a good-looking Joe Cool skirt-chaser who tip-toed a bit over the "line" of good taste in those years.

Or maybe he was simply an average, lonely, unsuspecting Joe Jerk who had one too many and thought - sadly as it turned out - that he'd gotten one-time "lucky" that night.

Some said it was at the bar of the swanky Magnolia Club on the corner of Main and Perry that they got together. But it just as easily could have been at Bishop's Bar on the other corner of Perry Avenue. Or it might have been at Jim

Miller's Flamingo Bar and Lounge a few doors up on the other side of Main Street, or at the big Spanish Villa night club where Joe and Eddie's Restaurant is today.

Maybe they met at Bill William's Indian Mound Saloon or farther along Main Street at Staff's Rep Room Bar & Lounge. The point is there was no shortage of watering holes in downtown Fort Walton Beach in those years. A new guy in town could find trouble pretty easy if he didn't know how to stay out of it.

If the Sheriff's advertising salesman had been a "local" he'd have known. After the evening gets rolling in a military town, any female not hooked up to one of our Country's smooth talking heroes is likely to be a couple of warts short of a swamp frog.

Trouble is, to a new guy on the block, those   warts may not show up right away..., especially when the Jack Daniels fog starts rolling in.

By all accounts, though, warts or no warts, they must have hit it off pretty well. For a tiny town, Main Street had an air of spine tingling excitement, even when nothing much was going on. There was something about it to set spirits and hungers churning. Palm trees lined both sides and the ocean breeze made their fronds dance and beckon. After other stores closed, windows and insides were dim, shadowy.

It was then that whiskey signs, willowy tubes of neon, gently painted the dark with cheerful color...red, green, gold, blue, white. Shimmering through the palms, they gave the night a sense of mystery and intrigue, far different from the parching heat of day.

Sidewalks, shadowed by rustling palms, the veiled flaxen glow of a street light here and there, clutched an intriguing, lonely sense of the night-shaded sea.

Inside, behind the glowing neon, was soft light and music, gleaming mahogany, companionship, laughter, warmth in the gut that made the world, for a while at least, a happy place.

Hours later, back out on the sidewalk in dawn's early hours, how good and fresh, how clean and cool, was Main Street's sea-scented breeze.

Maybe they covered them all, drifting from bar to bar.

That's pretty much how the Playground Area - oops, the Emerald Coast - partying crowd partied in the '50's. They usually ended up at Bill Williams' Indian Mound Saloon. It was the only place that partied 'til the roosters crowed. The others shut down around 2:00 a.m. or so.

That night, though, it's not likely the new couple made it to the Indian Mound's late night hurrah. By the morning's wee hours they were enjoying the sea and stars far outside city lights.

Highway 98, brightened only by the whims of nature, was a lonely way, except to those who reveled in it's solitude. After 9:00 or 10:00 in the evening, a car was a rare happening along the six miles or so to Destin. In the sea wind, headlights often surprised white sand clandestinely drifting out into rippled little gatherings in the dark roadway.

It was an every night thing to see white fiddler crabs scuttling over the black top in the bright, on-rushing glow of car lights. In the shadow of starlight, sand dunes along the beach loomed like pale ghosts. Bathed in moonlight, they took on a glow of their own, as though modest knolls, like rainbow's ends, were heaps of silver where moonbeams cascaded onto earth.

As it turned out, there's little doubt the new couple was seeking that solitude. On the hushed, secluded shores of East Pass, at the West end of Destin's bridge, was a small, aged cottage. It had been a little saloon, closed for a time, ruffled by neglect and the constant sea wind. It's dusty, crushed shell parking lot reached near the flowing, wind-rippled, waters of the Pass. In night hours, minuscule glows from a handful of back door night lights, guardians of the piers on Destin's harbor, twinkled warmth and welcome across blue-green water.

It was there, in that beguiling milieu of amour, on someone's blanket, that the hours-old friendship bloomed, for a while at least..., before something, somehow, went tempestuously awry.

Truth is, it's hard to imagine what Joe Cool could possibly have done, at the melting point they reached, to vex, to forfeit, to twist the ardent to rage, to exact such an explosive repartee.

Maybe he talked her into going "skinny dipping," then prodded for a bit too much. "Skinny dipping" was a wished-for dating venture a lot of wise guys smirked and bragged about. But we never knew of anyone who would actually admit doing it.

Anyway..., his new-found, almost-amour's, leaving was likely far more than unexpected. Perhaps reckless was a much better portrayal of it.

And, as it turned out, her teeth were splendidly sharp.

When she departed, the beach blanket, the car keys, the car, her clothes and...of all things, his... bolted away with her.

Six miles away down dark, lonely Highway 98, just across the John T. Brooks bridge, barely in downtown Fort Walton Beach, was a Billups gas station. It stood for a long, long time, always open all night, on the southeast corner of Main Street and Perry Avenue.

Under Billup's bright lights she screeched to a stop in someone's car...perhaps his, perhaps hers?... threw open the door, bounded to the concrete pavement next to the gas pumps.

Now, let's be fair to the lone, venerable, sleepy, all-night, station attendant. It's not surprising he was suddenly wide awake, goggle-eyed. After all, it's not everyday an old gent is suddenly confronted by a "lady", gleaming bare-nekkid as a jaybird, we used to say - hissing angry, hot-footing it towards the public bathroom, attire in hand.

Over her shoulder she snarled an order to call the sheriff to go out and get that "jerk" at Destin's bridge.

It's likely the salesman had quite a wait, in the cool expose of late-night hours, to ponder his mortifying dilemma, his faux pas..., whatever it might have been.

The sheriff had to come 30 miles..., all the way from Crestview, in those years to answer a call in tiny Fort Walton Beach or, far tinier, Destin.

What he found produced quite a few guffaws along the Main Street of Fort Walton Beach the next day.

But, the nightmare of it was enough to make a "ladies man" shiver. A few of them, it seems, gave serious thought, for a moment or two perhaps, to their way of life.

For what the sheriff's deputy came upon was Joe Cool standing gloomily by the side of a dark, lonely highway 98, not far from the Destin bridge.

Far more than unlucky at amour, the hapless swashbuckler was bare-arsed as the day he was born, bleeding bountifully from an impetuous gnash of teeth, his nose deeply slashed. In fact as "they" told it, the end of his nose was near gnawed off.

In a way, though, things could have been...well..., a wee bit worse.

Happily..., to an awfully slim degree, of course..., there was the papery thin, aluminum foil, pie pan. By some stroke of good fortune, thrown away on the roadside.

In dark, chastened moments it was, at least, a dinky shelter of sorts..., for you see it was held gingerly, rather humbly by then, in front of...well, you know where!

And..., he had a thumb stuck out, pointed toward town, hitching for a ride.

The burning question, the thing a lot of Main Street sports whispered about for a long time, though, was why Joe Cool thought anyone might pick him up.

History, to be sure - at least the retelling of it - can be a fickle, patronizing affair, a selective thing. It is indulgent, inordinately human, to record only the righteous, the cheerful, the splendid.

Truth is the nutty, the curious, the faltered, the fallen, the truly bad... are surely a part of it, a part of us.

On the Emerald Coast, in the comings and goings of our nomadic compatriots, we've seen it, touched it, experienced it all.

Maybe it's sufficient to remember it...some of it, at least...just the way it was.

About The Author

Jim Keir Baughman

ABOUT THE AUTHOR

JAMES KEIR BAUGHMAN

IN JULY OF 1949, on a two week military sojourn, James Keir Baughman became enamored of the beautiful area he writes about. Near the same time his family bought acreage at Miramar Beach in South Walton County, just east of Fort Walton Beach.

On June 1st, 1951 his parents Elba A. and Iris Keir Armour Baughman invested in a small conglomerate of retail businesses in Shalimar, a suburb of Fort Walton Beach, and moved the family there. He was 18 years old.

For the ensuing 52 years the author has been a joyful conspirator, sharing on a work-a-day basis the developmental history, the evolution of Florida's Great Northwest. It was the Playground Area when he came, then for long years the Miracle Strip, finally flourishing into America's luxurious new Riveria, Northwest Florida's magnificent Emerald Coast.

In vital formative years, the 1950's, 60's, and 70's, he knew personally all of those who are now locally famous, revered as Emerald Coast "pioneers." There are hundreds more, he notes, whose names are little known, folded silently in dusty files of local history.

The author ventured at Fort Walton Beach's weekly

Playground News from 1956 to1959, as ad salesman, advertising manager, columnist, and writer. That small town newspaper was one of Florida's finest then, grown now into the grandiose Northwest Florida Daily News. He served 10 1/2 years as a Fort Walton Beach City Councilman, one year as Mayor Pro Tempore.

Over the years, he served on Boards of Directors for the JayCees, Northwest Florida Regional Planning Council, Playground Area Safety Council, YMCA, Fort Walton Yacht Club, Holy Trinity Lutheran Church, Greater Fort Walton Beach Chamber of Commerce, Fort Walton Beach Downtown Merchants Assn, as a management advisor for Junior Achievement, as a Lieutenant in the Navarre Squadron of the Civil Air Patrol, and was active in the Florida League of Cities, and the Rotary and Lions clubs.

As a JayCee, he strived in the early development of the Emerald Coast's famous Billy Bowlegs Festival. His mother Iris Keir Armour Baughman guided the Greater Fort Walton Beach Chamber of Commerce for 14 years as Executive Director. He and his family members have owned ten business enterprises over the 52 year span.

During an extensive career in business management, sales, and advertising he published thousands of lines of copy as an advertising copywriter. In retirement he has enjoyed success, but - like most writers - minuscule financial reward, as a published writer in national and regional magazines of the condo management and sailing genre.

The author's love of sailing began five decades ago when he found the area's elegant, ocean and inland, emerald hued waters. He and his wife Sandee live ashore of Northwest's Florida's measure of the Gulf Coast Intra-Coastal Waterway reaching 800 miles through five states to the Mexican border. His children: James and wife Diane, Jill, Dana and husband Brent, are all professionals or business owners who pursue his enchantment with the delightful Emerald Coast lifestyle.

Few writers now have lived it...knew personally the people, the events, the hopes and dreams, the developmental years, the history of what has become the splendid Emerald Coast of Northwest Florida..., of America..., of the World.

Printed in the United States
50957LVS00003B/184